Perfect
In-House
Training

Perfect In-House Training

ALL YOU NEED
TO GET IT RIGHT
FIRST TIME

COLIN JONES-EVANS

ARROW

Published by Arrow Books in 1997

1 3 5 7 9 10 8 6 4 2

© Colin Jones-Evans 1997

First published by
Arrow Books Limited
20 Vauxhall Bridge Road, London SW1V 2SA

Random House Australia (Pty) Limited
16 Dalmore Drive, Scoresby, Victoria 3179, Australia

Random House New Zealand Limited
18 Poland Road, Glenfield
Auckland 10, New Zealand

Random House South Africa (Pty) Limited
Endulini, 5a Jubilee Road, Parktown 2193, South Africa

Papers used by Random House UK Limited are natural, recyclable products made from wood grown in sustainable forests. The manufacturing processes conform to the environmental regulations of the country of origin.

Companies, institutions and other organizations wishing to make bulk purchases of any business books published by Random House should contact their local bookstore or Random House Direct:
Special Sales Director
Random House
20 Vauxhall Bridge Road
London SW1V 2SA
Tel: 0171 973 9000 Fax: 0171 828 6681

Random House UK Limited Reg. No. 954009
ISBN 0 09 917572 X

Set in Bembo by
SX Composing DTP, Rayleigh, Essex
Printed and bound in Great Britain by
Cox & Wyman Ltd., Reading, Berkshire

British Cataloguing in Publication Data
A catalogue record for this book is available from the British Library

DEDICATION

To my wife Val, who supported and encouraged me throughout the writing of this book, and to my son Oliver who reminds me how exciting learning is. To my clients, who have allowed me to experiment, and have welcomed different ideas. To my fellow consultants who have worked with me on courses and helped me develop new approaches to training.

ACKNOWLEDGEMENTS

Thanks go to Lulu Bogue for administrative support; and to Janet Thompson, Kathryn Harris, and Jane Calverley, for giving their feedback and suggestions to improve this book. Finally, thanks to Dr Peter Honey for his permission to use the Honey and Mumford learning style model.

ABOUT THE AUTHOR

Colin Jones-Evans is a director of Virtua, consultants in management development and training. His work includes creating and running business simulations; and developing and running courses covering negotiating, influencing and consulting skills, interviewing techniques and team building. He has worked as a senior manager with Ernst & Young management consultancy and for BP. He runs management courses in a wide range of industry sectors in the UK and internationally, and is always delighted to consider new work in interesting organizations or countries. He can be contacted on:

Telephone: +44 (0) 181 224 2156
Fax: +44 (0) 181 224 2172
E-Mail: 100115.206@CompuServe.Com

CONTENTS

WHY USE A COURSE?

WHY IS LEARNING IMPORTANT?

'In the next decade we shall see changes in organizations that are greater than at any time in the past.' This statement could have been made at any time – by a Victorian industrial entrepreneur, or by a software corporate boss in the 1990s. I've certainly never heard anyone saying that change will be *slower* than before!

The changing environment for organizations and for their people means new learning. For organizations, change is prompted by technology, new trade markets, social trends, new competition, and new organization structures such as flatter or virtual structures. For people, change is prompted by the way their organizations respond to the outside world, and to what happens to them as they go about their work and their careers. People move jobs, change the way they do tasks, and become members of new teams as members come and go. This inevitably means that the way they behave, comprehend, or feel about things needs to change too.

Who is responsible for training?

'Those who can, teach; those who can't teach, end up having to do everything themselves.'

Managers in organizations are responsible for meeting present goals, but also for ensuring that they have the resources to meet their future goals. Most organizations spend as much money on people as they do in investing in buildings and equipment. And just as a building or a computer may need upgrading as demands change, so do people. For people, the process of upgrading is learning.

Learning can be planned or coincidental. It can be left to

the individual, who ensures they are gaining skills for their careers; or it can be controlled by the employing organization, which ensures that employees have the skills and knowledge to carry out the business plans. In fact, the healthiest form of learning is driven by both parties for both reasons: career and job requirements.

MAKING LEARNING HAPPEN

But how can an organization help someone to learn? An obvious solution, and the one this book is focused on, is running a course to meet the need. But there are a number of options for creating learning which should be considered before deciding to run a course.

Coaching

This is excellent for one-on-one learning. A manager or co-worker can coach someone to learn new skills by directing their efforts, giving them feedback and encouraging them on the job. This does assume that the person doing the coaching has the skills to do it positively and efficiently, that making mistakes on the job is all right, or that the coach can correct things before they become critical. This is perhaps why we never get introduced to a surgeon . . . and his coach!

Open or distance learning

Open learning and distance learning differ slightly. They can both be a cost-effective way of delivering knowledge-based learning, and sometimes skills at a time and a place convenient to the individual.

Open learning can be started at any time and at pace to suit. It may be done at an 'open learning centre' or anywhere the individual chooses, depending on what equipment is needed.

Distance learning differs slightly in that the learners are usually remote from each other, and from their 'teacher'.

They may start the same course together and follow it at the same pace, or again, start at different times.

The method of delivery may be a book (like this one), a computer disk or CD-ROM (also known as CDi), workbooks, video or audio tapes, or computer conferencing. The learning needs must be sufficiently widespread to justify these methods of delivery. An effective programme takes a long time to prepare. Consequently, open and distance learning is often of the generic variety – PC skills, bookkeeping, business management. There are many public and private sector providers of open and distance learning, the most famous being the Open University.

External courses
Like open learning, external courses are usually of a generic nature. They are not connected to an employing organization's goals, culture or skill sets in any way other than by careful selection of the course that most closely meets the employer's and the individual's needs. Another disadvantage is that external courses are rarely running at the best time to suit the person.

An advantage of external courses is that participants get to meet people in other industries, or firms; and they may feel more able to learn when they are away from their workplace and their colleagues.

In-house training
When you have sufficient numbers to justify a course, it can provide a specific solution to the needs of the organization sponsoring it, and to the individuals attending it.

When is in-house training worthwhile – Consider in-house training if you:

- Have enough people who need training at the same time. Depending on the nature of the course, anything from four people upwards may justify an in-house course.

- Have a group of people who work together that you want to train in one go so that they can reinforce each other's learning and become more of a team.

- Need to develop skills that are specific to the organization or to a group of jobs, either because of the organization's systems or methods, or because the uniqueness of the skills gives the organization a competitive edge.

- Want to foster the corporate culture on the course – 'the way we do things around here . . .'

- Would like the company to be more involved in the content of what is taught and the results of the training – the 'inputs' and the 'outputs'.

THE PROCESS OF IN-HOUSE TRAINING

How can you recognize a training need?

At an individual level. For a line manager, a training need may become most evident when a member of their staff is unable to perform to a required standard. The individual's 'skills gap' will probably be spotted after a few incidents of poor performance. Training is therefore to put things right and becomes an urgent need: not so much 'just in time' as 'better late than never'. Alternatively, the manager's members of staff may ask for training because it interests them, or they 'feel they need it'. Both of these sorts of training are driven from the bottom upwards – they help develop the individuals but they have few strategic links with the direction of the business.

For the job. As people move into different jobs they need to be prepared for them. This is another trigger for training. The job needs to be analyzed for the skills it requires and the level of performance which it requires against each skill. This analysis will yield a set of skills which can be grouped into competencies, for example: leading teams, copywriting, analyzing systems, or facilitating groups. Some competencies may be unique to a job, but many others will be common to that type or level of job. For example, all supervisors in a company might need to have skills of budget reporting, or using the company's time-recording system.

Knowing what is needed in a job enables a manager to assess someone's skills before they go into it and ensure they get trained to cover any skills gaps they may have.

Organizationally. For training to be integral to the business it must be considered against the organization's goals and the changing needs for skills. A training plan needs to be developed *from* the business plan highlighting:

- New skills needed resulting from changes to operations or new operations, e.g. setting up a customer technical help desk
- New skills needed as a result of new standards, e.g. improving levels of customer service
- Skills needed from changes to personnel in new roles due to turnover of staff, e.g. drawn from manpower plans
- Development of the 'skills pool' in line with future needs

A training plan will identify the broad groups of people that require such skills. Large organizations may need to break down their business plans into divisions or departments – then each of these also develops a training plan to complement its business plan. It is usually line managers who identify individuals against each category in need of the training.

Does everyone need to be trained?

To prevent the 'sheep-dip' approach to training, each individual needs to be assessed against the skills required from the training plan. This is often done at the time of personal appraisals, usually annually. More recently, many large organizations have started using 'development centres' to help identify people's existing skills and their needs for training.

What does this mean for line managers and trainers?

So how can line managers or trainers identify training needs? Here are some practical steps you can take to identify whether training is necessary and of what sort:

Look at the organizational needs

1   Look at your business plan.
2   What new demands will it place on existing staff?
3   What new skills will they require?
4   What are the existing skills you have in your area?
5   Which skills need to be recruited in, and which can be trained?
6   Even if you are recruiting from outside or promoting from within, what skills will those people need to fulfil the job requirements?
7   What alternatives are there for developing those skills?
8   Do you need a course?

Then look at a job level

1   What promotions or transfers require people to be doing things different from their old jobs which they don't have the skills or knowledge to do, and therefore need training?
2   What transfers *may* take place leading to similar needs? If you have succession planning it should also look at the skills required and what needs to be fulfilled. This means that people will have the skills before they move into a new job rather than just after . . . or too late.
3   Can or should a job be broadened so that the job-holder can get more satisfaction from it? This job enrichment may require further skills.

Then at an individual level

1 Review your people's performance against their exist-ing job requirements. Is there a training need to fill a gap?
2 Review your people's future career hopes. Although you may not be planning for them to move into a spe-cific job through your succession plans, training may help to broaden their skills and make them more employable in the future i.e. (empowerment), or simply more flexible now.

Answer: Yes, we need a course!

So you've decided you need a course – a perfect one. The rest of this book takes you through the process of creating and delivering an in-house course. It starts with identifying what needs to learnt and finishes with evaluation of the programme. Each stage is inter-related through a process of evaluation. The diagram below shows the links between the stages.

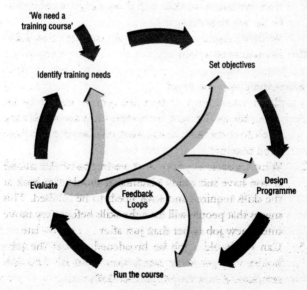

The training process

Don't assume that because you have run a successful course once that it will still meet the needs of the next participants. It's important to keep monitoring the needs and the design through the process of evaluation. Continuous improvement isn't just a matter of experimenting with the design – organizations move on and learning needs change.

Defining the aim of a course

The first step is defining the learning needs. I often find it helpful to have an overarching 'aim' for the course, which I will then break down further into objectives. Writing objectives is dealt with in the next chapter.

The statement of the aim gives a feel of the purpose and outcome of a course without going into specifics of what someone will be able to do. For example:

'Aim: to support the shift from a customer service group in which each person specializes in a product; to a team which pools its knowledge, with each individual able to deal with a customer's queries regardless of product.'

This is an example of an organizational change requiring change in a number of people. An example of a job-focused change might be:

'Aim: to gain the skills of being able to supervise junior staff by motivating them, delegating and monitoring their work, and coaching them where needed.'

But where will you find the sources of the aim and the objectives?

This depends largely on where the training need came from originally. If it is an organizational need – a change – then the sources will be in the minds of the architects of the change. Pin them down. What do they envisage as the jobs, role or culture that they are aiming for? Ask them what they think will be the various tasks which a person might need to do, how often they will do them, how important they are, and how complex. The most frequent, most important and most complex ones are those to focus on for in-depth training.

If the need is at a job level then the sources will be existing job descriptions and person specifications. Objectives specifically set for the job give a good indication of what it is about and the required level of mastery.

Now you have clarified the aim of the course and perhaps some initial objectives. The next chapter deals with gaining commitment from the people who will be supporting the training, and defining the objectives more carefully.

2

WHAT DO YOU WANT TO ACHIEVE?

'Would you tell me please which way I ought to walk from here?' said Alice. 'That depends a good deal on where you want to get to,' said the cat.

The most successful programmes have clear objectives that have been set before anything else is decided. Certainly my worst disasters have been when the purpose and objective of a course have been woolly or confused.

This chapter is about setting objectives:

- who sets them
- what is a good objective
- gaining management commitment to objectives
- ensuring objectives are realistic
- tailoring objectives to specific individuals

WHO POSITIONS THE GOAL POSTS?

A critical part of setting objectives has to be making sure that the right person is doing it. Training in organizations is usually done to help people achieve organizational goals. Who sets those? In some places you'd think it was the training department. This results in the sort of 'bottom up' training that is laudable but misguided. You know when you're running such a course, because participants say: 'that's all very well but my manager won't let me do that.' This means that the chances of new learning being supported and encouraged in the workplace are slim.

A course that is tied in with senior management's business goals is more likely to succeed, not only because they'll want to sponsor it, but because the outcomes of a course are more likely to be supported and reinforced by them.

If you are the manager who will be involved in reinforcing, rewarding and encouraging behaviours, great! You can clarify in your own mind what you want your people to do, know or value. If the 'sponsors' of the programme – those who want it to achieve things for their people – are not those delivering the training, then you need to gain their commitment and approval for its objectives.

GAINING MANAGEMENT COMMITMENT

Gaining management commitment to the objectives of a course can be done in a number of ways:

- involve them in the design
- ensure that the training solves the current problems as they see them
- get managers involved in the delivery of the training
- ask them how they will judge the success of a course

But how do you set the objectives of a course?

WHAT IS A GOOD OBJECTIVE?

Knowledge, Skills and Attitudes

An effective way of breaking down objectives into more measurable parts is to break them down into Knowledge, Skills and Attitudes (KSA):

Knowledge – information and understanding

Skills – the ability to do something

Attitude – an underlying belief or value

All three can to a greater or lesser extent, be tested. You may need to build this into the design of your course if you need to evaluate the course itself or the expected outcomes. (See chapter 9.)

By describing a course's objectives in terms of KSA it becomes easier to design its parts: each part has a clear purpose. In order to gain this clarity it is helpful to describe what participants will know (knowledge), be able to do (skills), or value (attitude). These are known as 'behavioural objectives'.

Writing behavioural objectives

Go for brevity and clarity when writing these. Here's an example from a restaurant's customer service course.

By the end of the course, participants will:

- know how to deal with complaints according to the company's policy *(knowledge)*
- be able to welcome a new customer in a friendly manner *(skills)*
- want to keep a customer happy *(attitude)*

From this you can see how it's fairly easy to test whether someone has achieved these, though measuring attitude is harder. Measuring someone's attitude or values is a complex task, often requiring surveys to be designed. Inferring attitude from behaviour may be easier. You may like to use some behavioural indicators of success as your measure instead of the attitude itself.

For example, instead of 'want to keep customer happy' you might have:

- will apologize for errors clearly and sincerely without prompting
- will offer options to the customer to put things right

ARE YOUR OBJECTIVES ACHIEVABLE?

If you are not sponsoring the course, get agreement to these objectives from the sponsors. But before you offer the earth, have a reality check: are these objectives possible?

On occasions I've been roped into doing work which I should never have agreed to. It's flattering to be asked to do challenging work. But as the project has progressed I've realized that the goal is an impossible dream, and the further I've got into the project without saying 'stop', the more I have 'colluded' with the sponsor. Reasons why something may be over-ambitious include:

- you haven't got the skills to design or deliver the course
- the participants' existing capabilities or skills are too low
- the resource constraints for the course are too great (not enough time, budget, people)
- managers aren't ready for the demands made of them and consequently will undermine the course when people return

TAILORING OBJECTIVES TO YOUR PARTICIPANTS

When making presentations, there is the old adage that there are three considerations: audience, audience and audience. Training is identical. The emphasis of training philosophy has in recent years become more 'learner centred'. This is important for many reasons: it takes us away from the sheep-dip mentality (or blanket approach); it makes us consider different learners, and it makes us think how we are helping people to learn (the process) as well as what they are learning (the content).

The issues of *how* people learn are dealt with in chapter 4 but in this chapter we should look at how participants influence the content objectives.

Firstly, are you considering a mixed group or a uniform/homogeneous one? The mix may be on the basis of seniority, job type, or existing skill level. There are benefits accruing from both mixed and similar approaches.

- Groups of similar people allow a simpler and narrower design because existing skills or target skills are shared
- Mixed groups provide a more organizational benefit because they can enable participants to see what people do and think in other jobs or levels of seniority, or within their teams

If the overall pool of people from which you are drawing your participants is small then you are probably going to have mixed groups.

If you have mixed groups, it may be useful to write different objectives for the various types within each group. These objectives may vary slightly around an issue or dramatically according to role. For example, the difference between a team member and supervisor on an issue of customer care may be just that the team member handles initial problems and the supervisor ensures that they are handled properly, and acts as reference if necessary. The skills you want the people to learn may remain the same; the point at which the skills are employed can vary.

Much of the training I do is designed for a broad crosssection of people, but occasionally I'm asked to design something for a group where every person has very specific needs. I've been in the situation when a manager has told me that he wants each person in a group of twenty people to learn very different things, in a day! This is both an extreme, and an impossible task, unless every person had virtually one-to-one coaching. When faced with demands such as this, I am inclined to think that this is not a training issue, but a coaching one.

Training courses need to have broadly similar objectives for participants. This enables them to be mentally engaged throughout the course. If people are only learning for a fraction of the time, they switch off, or keep themselves involved throughout other activities, like trying to influence a change in the design of the course. Inputs, exercises and discussions need to be able to be linked to the work context – this is how adults learn best. For a mixed group this may mean that you need to create exercises broad enough to make sense to everyone.

Where you can help participants on the course is to enable them to relate those common materials, general discussions and exercises to their various different roles and jobs. It is fine to tailor material for your participants so that they can relate it to the content of their work, but beware the multi-headed monster where you are being asked to run a dozen different courses at the same time.

The setting of objectives is only one part of the equation. To ensure that participants *and* the organization can bene-fit from a course you need to think of the wider context. An off-the-job course needs a lot more linking to make it work than coaching someone in the job itself. The next chapter looks at what you can do to ensure a better fit with the organization.

3

MAKING SURE A COURSE FITS WITH YOUR ORGANIZATION

Courses can be standalone or integrated into an organization so that they create the changes needed. Changing an individual is rarely sufficient; people prefer you to be predictable. This means that if someone attempts to change, the behaviour pattern of other people may well remain fixed and prevent it from happening.

For example, a manager with a tendency to blow up at his staff went on a management skills course and learned to control his temper and consult his staff. At the end of the course he was a changed man. But a couple of months later he found that his staff were still avoiding him. When the trainer asked a couple of them what they had noticed after he returned they said: 'he's been bottling things up so much since the programme that we're certainly not going to be around when he finally explodes!'

The problem was not one of the manager's making; it was because his staff were as much a part of the problem as his behaviour before the course. Had the situation continued any longer before the trainer intervened as an 'organizational consultant' by talking to the staff, we might well have been back where we started. The manager's staff were reinforcing his old behaviours. By assuming the behaviours would continue, the staff might have pushed their manager into a frustrated state, and got confirmation that their beliefs were right all along!

HELPING LEARNERS TO TRANSFER THEIR LEARNING

Once you have considered what else is affecting the individual you can start to identify ways of helping them to transfer their learning into the workplace. If your course is standalone then you might not be able to intervene in the workplace, so assisting the transfer has to be done on the course. You could do this by:

- Working with the learner to identify what might go wrong and develop strategies to overcome it
- Encourage 'over-learning' which helps the learner to maintain new behaviour without reinforcement. This requires a longer course so that a learner can get in a lot of practice, which enables them to make responses which are automatic, rather than needing reinforcement
- Rehearse a challenging situation with learners so that they can 'automate' some of their new learned behaviours in a realistic environment. This gives them many of the triggers which might prompt old behaviours, but instead of relapsing they can learn how to change the response to something they feel would be more effective
- Encourage course participants to support and reinforce each other's behaviour after a course. This is easier if they work together. If not, they could agree to follow up their learning with a meeting to rehearse difficult situations, problem-solve, or discuss what went wrong with something and what they might do differently

WORK GROUPS – HELPING THE ORGANIZATION TO HELP LEARNERS

If you do have access to a learner's workplace then you can work with others to ensure that their learning fits even better. Questions to ask yourself include:

- How can I involve the learner's work group – colleagues, clients, manager(s) and subordinates – before, during and after a course?
- What is the degree of need for any changes and where is the support to be found?
- How will a change affect others in the work group?

- How much does the work group know about likely change in the learner, and how do they perceive the impact of this change?

Before a course

A trainer can get a work group to help a learner by involving them early on. Ideas include:

- The work group identifies what has to be learned and how they will know whether it has been successful
- The work group gives feedback on existing skills and abilities, through detailed surveys, open-ended questionnaires, or discussions with the learner
- The manager creates a project and task for the learner – to be started after the course – which is designed to use the newly learned skills

Pre-course preparation of this kind gives a much stronger impetus for an individual to learn. When I have run consulting skills courses that use pre-course questionnaires answered by clients, course participants have gained much encouragement from their clients' feedback. It has caused them to wonder why clients have said some things and how the participants can work with the client differently. Questionnaires like this can help by opening up a discussion between a learner and someone with whom they work about what they do, how they do it, and what the other person likes or dislikes.

There is also a degree of neutrality about a questionnaire which a face to face discussion frequently lacks. As pre-work for an 'influencing skills' course we encourage participants to send a questionnaire to people with whom they have difficult relationships (as well as good ones). Almost 100 per cent of the time they pluck up the courage to do it. As a result they get valuable feedback from the people they feel least able to ask a direct question.

Not only do participants benefit directly from this information, but because a learner's work group has had early
involvement the work group's expectancy for change is
stimulated. A small and helpful change can be initiated just
by involving the work group *before* a course.

During a course

Work groups can help directly or indirectly in a course
itself. Directly, they might act as co-trainers or facilitators,
role-players or as fellow participants. Indirectly, they can
help in the design of the programme or write exercises from
their own experiences which give a realistic context to
role-plays.

As an external consultant many of my assumptions about
training course design are based on the organizations that I
already know. Different organizations have different cultures of learning. Even departments can vary.

Work groups, and particularly course sponsors, can act as an
important check on an external consultant's design to
ensure that it is acceptable and 'normal' in the organization's experience of learning. Only break away from the
'normal' if you know what effect you want to gain from it.

For example, if an organization's normal learning design
requires a trainer to give 'expert' feedback to participants
about how they did, then asking them to give each other
feedback may break with tradition and meet with resis-
tance. But if you want to encourage people to continue to
give feedback to each other after a course, say in teams, then
you might be justified in making this change to the learning culture. You are teaching people a different way of
learning, which helps their teams work better.

Learning culture can be influenced by the way training has
been conducted in the organization before, the type of
department or discipline people are working in, and the

broader national culture. The influence of national culture is covered in chapter 6.

After a course

When participants return to their work from a course, they often fail to implement learning if they:

- fail to get the opportunity to practise their skills
- find that their work groups treat them exactly as before
- get no follow-up of their learning, particularly from their manager, which could reinforce it

To avoid this you can either form a bridge between the course and participants or you can create a mechanism to encourage the right things outside the course.

The bridge with work could be created by inviting the participants' managers or work group members to join the end of a course and discuss its content and what needs to happen back at work to reinforce it. For example, a secretary's working relationship with her manager is usually very interdependent. The pattern of how they work together develops over time and can be hard to change. A secretarial course might be made more effective by inviting each secretary's manager to the course so the managers know not only what was discussed, but what was most important to their secretary and how it will affect the pattern of their teamwork.

4

DEVELOPING YOUR APPROACH

Developing a good programme and working with participants in an effective way demands that you know what your approach is and how to conduct yourself. Underpinning your approach is the *way* people learn. Knowing how to conduct yourself means that you have a grasp of the processes going on and how to respond positively and ethically.

This section presents some of the theories and ideas of learning and what the implications are for trainers. It then presents some practical guidelines which allow for best learning. If you treat these as your own rules it's a lot easier to carry out your task ethically.

Remember, the theories and beliefs are based on generalizations about behaviour, personality and learning. As a result, not everything will apply to your participants, who are all different and (usually) want to be treated as such. Always be adaptable.

HOW PEOPLE LEARN

Behavioural approaches

From birth we learn in many different contexts. Early behavioural research focused on the external control of learning, the most famous works being those of Pavlov and Skinner.

Pavlov's dog salivated whenever a bell was rung, because the dog was taught to associate the bell with food arriving. The salivating continued when the bell rang even though food no longer arrived. The bell was known as *stimulus* and the salivating as *response*. The way in which they become linked was termed *classical conditioning*.

Skinner's rats were taught to operate a lever which reinforced the behaviour by releasing a reward – food. This is *operant conditioning* – learned by trial and error by a chance operation leading to a reinforcement.

This early behavioural research shows how the role of the trainer is important in ensuring that rewards are clearly linked to the required behaviour. Initially the reward might be praise given on a course. Later it needs to be on the job, by praise or by results – an intrinsic reward.

Humanistic approaches and learner-centred training

Later work by humanistic psychologists focused on the role of motivation to achieve an individual's potential. Work by Maslow on a hierarchy of human needs gives the ultimate drive to that of self-actualization; achieving one's own potential.

Carl Rogers, the father of the client–centred approach in counselling, showed that to achieve your own potential it is important to have help from someone who works with you in an accepting, feeling way. This client-centred approach has been translated directly into the training environment as the *learner-centred approach*. This approach has four tenets:

1 You can't teach someone directly; you can only facilitate their learning. Or alternatively: 'You can lead a horse to water but you can't make it drink.'
2 'A person learns significantly only those things which he perceives as being involved in the structure of self.' Or: 'What's in it for me.'
3 Significant learning is resisted. Or: 'This is too much to handle.' Major learning may result in someone having to completely rethink their ideas and beliefs, so the person protects their existing beliefs by blocking the new ideas.

4   The most effective, significant learning setting allows for:

- the threat to the self to be reduced to a minimum
- facilitation of learning rather than forced teaching

Carl Rogers has been extremely influential. His ideas permeate most management, training and counselling approaches, leading to worker participation, autonomous work groups and many of the ground rules that trainers take for granted.

Rules covering both physical and emotional safety are important, and rules which allow for learners to have some autonomy give a greater feeling of the learning being for their self-development. Some guidelines for effective learning include:

Confidentiality – keep what happens on a course confidential from outsiders. Make it known to a group and agree it with them.

Safety – no physical risk of harm to participants.

Responsibility – participants have responsibility for their learning. The trainer has responsibility for the environment and the resources including content. If a participant finds he isn't learning, it's up to him to say what he needs and for the trainer to act on it.

Autonomy – it's OK to opt out of an activity if it feels too risky, either physically or emotionally.

METHODS OF LEARNING AND THE LEARNING CYCLE

Participants prefer to learn in different ways. Some prefer to get stuck into activities and experiment; others like to read the underpinning theory to help them understand. Knowing what your participants favour can help you to design the most helpful approach for them. You might discover this by using a pre-course questionnaire, or if your course is one in a series with the same group you could discuss their preferred learning styles on the first pro-gramme. But it is also important to help people learn by giving them a variety of learning approaches which help to reinforce the learning objectives, so don't concentrate on only one learning method.

Peter Honey and Alan Mumford devised a useful model which reflects the various preferences. The learning cycle covers four phases:

Activity – experimentation through exercises or trying out ideas

Analysis – reflecting on what happened and why

Concepts – the theories that explain and predict

Connections – making links with what happens in 'real life'

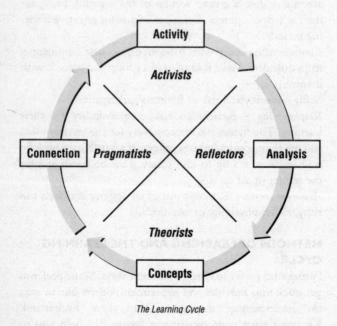

The Learning Cycle

Source: Honey and Mumford

The main idea of the theory is that people need to follow

through the cycle to learn most effectively, but that they want to emphasize different parts according to their preference. For a trainer the implications are that your design for learning needs to encompass all four parts. Unless you know in advance what the various members of a group prefer, you'll probably spend roughly equal time on each activity, but build in some flexibility for different parts.

There are four learning styles. Each needs different learning methods.

Activists – will want to get into activities on a course as soon as possible. Equally they may like to be drawn in to spontaneous activities like role plays, while others – especially the reflectors – look on.

Reflectors – may need longer to prepare for and review activities. They may also value an opportunity to make sense of things, so making yourself available to them out of hours is helpful.

Theorists – might be encouraged to do extra study outside a course after concepts have been discussed or provided to the group.

Pragmatists – might need to spend more time discussing implications for work and how ideas link to their experiences. So making connections could be started in the group (as everyone needs it) and continued during breaks in a more informal way.

There is a flip side to this. You as a trainer may instinctively recognize your preferred style. If not, Honey and Mumford's book contains a learning questionnaire which will help you identify it. You may subconsciously place greater emphasis on some parts of the cycle more than others. Being aware of your learning style will help you ensure a balanced approach.

Spacing and grouping

As well as designing activities to meet individual preferences we need to help people to remember what they learn. As a trainer two questions which arise are:

- Should you break up the learning into spaced modules or do it in one go?
- Should you break down the tasks into smaller sub-tasks or get people to try the whole thing?

Research into learning has also focused on the effectiveness of whole or part learning; and on block compared with spaced learning. Some research has been inconclusive, but there is general agreement that spaced learning, allowing rests between practising skills, gives rise to better performance and greater recall.

The importance of context

Adults like to know what the value of learning is. If a session in a company course you were attending was entitled 'Esperanto Part I' your first question would probably be 'what has this got to do with my job?' If it was positioned correctly and a strong link was made with your job and how it would enable you to perform it better, then you might be more likely to accept it. Equally, practice of a skill or use of new knowledge is more effective when it is performed in an environment, or context, similar to the learner's job.

Providing a realistic context for learning a skill helps the learner. The greatest and most powerful context is train on-the-job, but as a training course is usually off-the-job, the challenge for the trainer is to make the context realistic.

WHAT'S IN A NAME?

Whether you are held in awe for your knowledge or regarded as being just someone who keeps things going smoothly, what you do influences a group. Equally, the role you are perceived to be performing is influenced by what people know or hear about you before a course, what they see of you during it and how you *present* your role.

Titles can influence perceptions. Do you call yourself a trainer, instructor, facilitator, consultant, teacher, course manager, director, chairman or nothing at all? What do the names imply? The short answer is that they probably imply what the participants take them to imply. Even if you call yourself an instructor, if you avoid giving any directions and use only questioning, participants may soon change their views about what role you are playing. But it may help to choose a title that clarifies your role early on, and then describe what your role is, and whether it might change.

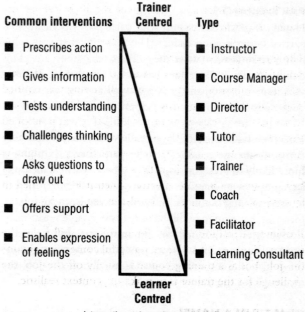

Common interventions	Trainer Centred	Type
■ Prescribes action		■ Instructor
■ Gives information		■ Course Manager
■ Tests understanding		■ Director
■ Challenges thinking		■ Tutor
■ Asks questions to draw out		■ Trainer
■ Offers support		■ Coach
■ Enables expression of feelings		■ Facilitator
	Learner Centred	■ Learning Consultant

Intervention styles and types of trainers

The actual role you choose depends on how much the course is being driven by the organization's needs and how much on the individual learner's. Consider these examples:

- A safety procedures course has to ensure a certain level of knowledge or skill. Whilst you may facilitate a good learning environment, you are unlikely to be able to offer options for what people learn. You will be adopting an **instructor-led** role to ensure quality and consistency of learning.
- Enlightened organizations may provide self-development programmes for their staff that allow them to consider their career and life in the broadest sense. In this case, they need to have a **facilitated approach** to learning – they can't be instructed how to live their lives.

YOUR RELATIONSHIP WITH COURSE PARTICIPANTS

Having a good relationship with participants is an integral part of being a good trainer. Demonstrate that you value them, regardless of what they do or what they are. This doesn't mean that a trainer has to be a pushover, but that you respect participants' rights as well as your own. Your purpose is to help in their development.

You may have certain responsibilities to their employing company for the conduct of your participants. Nothing is more likely to give you angst than when a participant damages property, themselves or someone else. The days of free booze and long nights on residential courses are long gone for most, but you may still be in the unenviable position, as I have been, of having to admonish participants after a riotous evening. And they are not always the more junior ones! If it all goes wrong, see 'Taking action over misdemeanours' on p.33.

A trainer is in a special position of authority, even when he or she is more junior than the participants. Because of that position, during longer courses a group tends to go through a number of phases in their relationship with a trainer:

Dependency – Initially everything you say is taken as gospel. Participants depend on you for everything and expect you to be able to solve their toughest problems at a stroke. It sounds like heaven to many, but it isn't a healthy position to learn in. The trainer ends up with responsibility for learning instead of the learner.

Counter-dependency – Inevitably you fall (or are pushed!) off your pedestal and participants start to lose faith. They start laying traps for you. They may question your views in detail to test your knowledge, or give you impossible questions. They identify you as an organizational lackey, then remind you how badly things are run. This is usually the low point of a course.

Inter-dependency – If you continue to demonstrate your interest in them and continue to help them to learn, participants will take on the mantle of responsibility for their learning. They will treat you as an equal, coming to you for advice about how they are learning when they need it. The emphasis here is on shared control.

The challenge for trainers is to help the group move through these stages as quickly as possible. Awkward as it may seem, it often helps to avoid feeding the participants' dependency. This moves them out of the dependency phase faster.

Consult them about the way they prefer to do something. Share control early. Try not to answer all their questions yourself. Ask further questions to guide them towards solutions themselves, or throw some questions to other members of their group: 'John, you've worked in that field, what has worked for you?' This starts fostering a belief within the group that it is able to solve its own problems.

When you are getting signals of counter-dependency, don't

despair (or get your coat). Keep faith in yourself and above all else, keep faith in your group.

The more you can do early on to signal your sharing of control and responsibility, the easier this is to achieve.

Lackeys, mavericks and optimists

To what extent are you going to toe the line? Being part of an organization or running one of its courses may mean that you are expected to take the management view (even if you aren't one yourself). Or if you set yourself up as a maverick what effect will this have on participants?

Both extremes have their advantages. Taking the management line enables the organization to reinforce its ideal culture, the one it wants to develop. A maverick approach encourages people to step outside their normal mould of thinking, to question taboo subjects and to demand change on their return to work.

But both tend to have a major disadvantage: are they really focused on the interests of the individual participants and helping them to learn?

The third, and middle position, is one in which you acknowledge the various inconsistent messages thrown out by the organization and the bad practices of the managers using the Genghis Khan management style. After all, name one good company that adheres to *all* its policies and practices, amongst *all* its managers – then still gets participants to aspire to follow best practice! Taking this line requires realism and positivism, looking for solutions rather than reasons we can't achieve something. A trainer's response to a participant might be: 'We can't fix everything through a course, but we can fix some things, so let's see how it can be done.'

Rules, rules, rules

No matter what style you employ, trainers still have to

uphold company policy, both for themselves and for participants. This includes policy towards safety, sexual and racial equality, anti-social behaviour, drink and drugs abuse, and any other things that go on when you have a bunch of people working in close proximity over extended periods.

As well as being a learning facilitator, a trainer sometimes has to be both manager and policeman to ensure the well-being of the participants.

Know the company rules and procedures if things go wrong. But most of all, think defensively: how can you prevent accidents or incidents happening in the first place?

Safety
Office or hotel venues
Make sure participants know the basic safety rules for the site where the course is. If there is a fire, for example, as a trainer you may be responsible for making sure everyone is evacuated. Let them know:

- where the exits are
- what to do if a fire is discovered
- where to assemble

Outdoors, offshore, and other higher risk environments
These will have many other safety requirements. Make sure someone is on hand to ensure safe operations. If you have selected the venue where activities themselves may be risky, make sure you or a more knowledgeable colleague do a safety assessment. Your own company safety officer should be able to help. Remember that participants may not always be in peak health or fully mobile. If the venue or activities require a level of fitness above that required of their normal jobs, this should be made clear, and a fitness assessment may be required. Accidents happen either because safety standards have not been present, precautions have been

ignored, or because someone's health is not up to the additional demands of a training activity.

If any of this puts you off outdoor training, then good. It is a valuable context for many participants, but must be carefully approached.

When looking at outdoor training centres, ask to speak to the centre's safety manager, and ask for the safety policy and certification. If any is absent, you may be taking unnecessary risks. Try somewhere else.

Alcohol

In many Western cultures alcohol has played a part in courses. Many people have stories of late-night binges and blurry Friday mornings when participants arrived looking like death, or didn't arrive until well into the morning. For some, this is the attraction of a course, especially if the company is paying!

If this happened at work, employees might find themselves having to explain their poor performance to their managers and undergoing a disciplinary procedure. Unless a course is paid for by a participant and takes place in their own time, their behaviour is subject to the usual company standards. The trainer is usually the person responsible for ensuring company standards are maintained.

If a course has genuinely been set up for learning then the excessive consumption of alcohol doesn't help. Out of hours it may lead to breaches in safety rules (glasses falling into a swimming pool, drinking in the sauna etc.), or unacceptable behaviour (arguments, fights, careless and hurtful remarks). In class it reduces attention span, motivation, ability to think, or just distorts behaviour so much that other participants won't want to work with someone. And the hungover participant will dismiss their behaviour as 'the drink talking'.

It does sometimes happen that a participant comes to a course with a pre-existing drink problem, and no one has done anything about it yet. But regardless of this, a trainer's actions have to be the same:

- try to prevent alcohol abuse before a course by limiting its availability
- remind participants of their responsibilities for their behaviour (misdemeanours are the one exception to confidentiality rules)
- take action swiftly and decisively if a breach occurs

Prevention is better than cure

You may be acting against the interests of a hotel who want to sell more alcohol but you need to be tough – you are paying the bill. Make sure that participants have plenty of water throughout the day. No one needs to have alcohol at lunch, so make sure it isn't available. If a hotel has a bar which can't be closed, don't encourage meeting in it before lunch; tell participants that refreshments will be provided at the lunch table (fruit juice or water), and certainly don't allow the company to pay for any lunchtime drinks at the bar. Limit the amount of wine over dinner. Don't allow late bar extensions for a course. These result in late-night drinking sessions.

And most importantly, make the rules clear at the beginning of the course.

Taking action over misdemeanours

Check before your course to see whether the company has any procedures for misdemeanours. There may be a procedure written for courses. If you have to take action follow the company's procedures. If there aren't any:

1 Investigate the incident by questioning any witnesses and noting down their responses
2 Interview the participant involved if you are satisfied

that the incident occurred, to hear their side. If you are
still reasonably certain that the incident took place, tell
the participant you are sending them back to work, and
why, and that you will be informing their line manager
3   Contact the line manager and the company training
     department and tell them of the events and your action
4   Write up all details as a file note and send one copy to
     the line manager, plus a copy to the training depart-
     ment
5   Keep a copy of your notes for use if you are called as a
     witness later. Further action will be up to the line man-
     ager.

If you prepare carefully, you are unlikely to have to ever do
this, but forewarned is forearmed.

Smoking

Whether to allow smoking on a course is becoming less of
an issue as more and more companies, like airlines, instigate
non-smoking policies. A course should follow the company's and/or the venue's guidelines on smoking if they
have them. If not, follow the preferences of the participants
or your own feelings. You may object strongly to smoking,
or may be desperate to smoke yourself! If you are ambiva-
lent, consider your participants. Many trainers opt for a
middle ground of no smoking in main rooms, but allow it
in syndicates provided the members agree. If you know of
participants who normally smoke, don't make it tougher on
them, check if they need breaks.

5

PREPARING FOR A COURSE

Clearly the amount of preparation you might have to do depends on the scope of the course. If you are running a major event with fifty participants and a training team of five, and will be using both indoors and outdoors, then you'll need to do a lot more than if you're running a one-hour workshop on your own with five participants.

For smaller sessions parts of this section may not apply. But for most courses, run in an office, a hotel or a conference venue, it contains tips covering everything up to when you're ready to kick off. There's a checklist at the end which can be photocopied.

Preparation covers three areas:

- Yourself (and the training team)
- Participants
- The venue

PREPARING YOURSELF (AND YOUR TEAM)

How much preparation you need may depend on how confident you feel in front of a group and how well you know your material. I've sometimes spent as long on the preparation for a course as on running it, or even longer. On other courses I can arrive and deliver something from memory without doing anything other than running through it in my head beforehand.

Team delivery is more complex. A team needs to present an integrated and united front to a participant so he or she can get on with what they are there for: to learn. There's nothing more disquieting to a participant than a team who seems to be at loggerheads, can't agree on the process, or has different ways of doing things.

Materials

Lectures, exercises, and games all require some content and a form. You may already have most of the materials you want for your course. Most trainers I know are great hoarders of such things. Over the years it is possible to build up a huge library which can be adapted for many things. Space is at a premium in most offices, so unless you have access to a good paper archiving system or don't mind cluttering up your loft with manuals, you'll probably find that you can't keep all those ring binders you've accumulated. And even if you can, you are unlikely to remember *all* the materials and where they are.

The earlier you can start developing a decent cataloguing system, the better. Then you can save just those pages which will remind you of the necessary facts or approach to running a session. The system I've adopted is to have a filing cabinet of folders arranged in subject order, which are then replicated on my computer's hard disk. For materials I've written or had retyped this then gives me a measure of search-ability by name, topic, date etc.

The hardest part is to create your original index of subjects. A library catalogue may help, or looking at a range of course indexes may also give you clues. Time devising a good catalogue is well spent, as it is harder to change it later than to get it right first time. Sharing materials expands your pool and the time you spend in researching materials. For instance, a training department could keep materials in a central pool and the team of trainers could have their computer files on a server so that all could access it.

Having selected materials you'll need to turn them into lecture notes or exercises. For yourself you need to have trainer notes (see p.39); for participants you may want handouts and visual aids. If you're running a course away from the workplace you should also consider other visual or tactile devices, such as samples, mock-ups, models and so on.

Participant Notes

Consider your preferred style for participant notes. Do you want full text (like this) or a few bullet-point notes as a reminder?

You may want to hand out your notes topic by topic. One word of warning though: if you have many sheets of handouts and a large group, loose sheets can be a problem. The course becomes more of a paper-handling exercise than a course, and participants soon become fed up with and distracted by passing around paper to their colleagues! As a trainer you'll also know the problems of turning up well before a course only to spend ages getting handouts in the right order. It might be a better idea to bind them together as a pack, and hand them out at the beginning of a course.

Spiral binding is less bulky but ring-binders allow extra notes to be put in, or pages to be removed. Double-sided copying is more environmentally friendly, but then consider where participants can make notes: a pad, blank pages at the back of their bound book, or space left on some pages where notes might come in handy.

If using spiral binding or ring-binders think carefully about how you are going to prevent participants from pre-empting you, reading exercise briefs in advance or just withdrawing from group discussions while they read everything cover to cover. I normally talk participants through a book so that they know what's there, and tell them that I'll keep them informed as to where we are in the book. If I use a manual with exercises I say I trust them not to read exercise briefs until the right time as it only spoils the exercise for them.

Overheads

If you are making larger presentations, or if company style is to use overhead projectors rather than flip charts, you have to produce overhead slides.

If you have a corporate style for overheads, great. Most of your thinking has been done for you. If not, make sure you have thought out your style for layout and that you and your colleagues stick to it rigidly. Here are a few rules of thumb:

- Typestyle should be consistent and clear. Minimum font size should be 36pt for main headings and 18pt for body text. That's at least ¼" (5mm) high or more for body text and bigger for main headings.

- Be clear and brief in your words. Avoid abstract nouns such as 'judgement', 'clarity', 'quality'. Try to keep bullets to one line and use similar language in each one.

- Keep graphics simple. Too many details are lost at the back of a room. If you need to convey detail use a handout.

- If colour is available, use bold, dark colours for text or graphics. Orange and yellow are usually hard to read, but can be good for backgrounds.

- Keep bullet points down to seven so that you don't have long and boring lists. If memory retention is important, limit them to five. Research into memory has shown that most people can hold only seven unrelated items in their memory, plus or minus two.

- Use the top two-thirds of your slide only. Stuff at the bottom either falls off the projector's platen or is blocked from view on the screen.

- Choose either portrait or landscape style orientation and stick to it. Keep your text and graphics within an imaginary 180mm by 200mm frame so that it doesn't slip off the platen.

An example of a slide:

PRODUCING OVERHEADS

- Text – consistent style
    – font 18pt or bigger
- Words – brief, simple and clear
- Use simple graphics
- Colours – bold and dark
- Seven bullets or less
- Use top two-thirds of slide only
- Portrait or landscape

Presentation Skills 5

Creating Trainers' Notes

Whether you are running a course on your own, in a team, or will be handing over to other trainers to run the same event in the future, you'll need some notes. The style and coverage of the notes will vary according to who you write for and how much control you want over every course session.

When I am running a course on my own I sometimes do some notes as a mind-map (see below). For a course which is being run by a team of people which varies over several events I would have a trainer manual which records every session clearly. Both approaches are detailed below so you can adapt something which suits you.

Personal Notes – It is important that you have clearly in your mind what the objectives are for each part of a course. But you also need a script so that you remember to say everything that's important but without repeating yourself. A script doesn't have to be word for word – in fact that would make for a very hard-to-follow set of notes and a potentially dull session – key words to prompt your natural speech are better.

Mind-mapping can be very helpful as a planning tool and set of notes. For a full description of mind-mapping see Tony Buzan's book, *Use Your Head*. The key to the mind-map is to set your central theme in the centre, then as you generate the contents, put the main themes on the main branches and sub-themes on sub-branches and twigs. You decide how much level of detail you need according to how good your recall is of the subject. When the mind-map is complete and put in order (clockwise) of the sessions or topics, you can add little logos to remind you to use a flip chart or overhead projector slide (OHP), or give a handout.

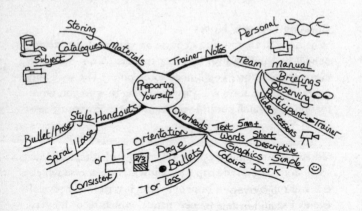

Team notes or manual – A manual serves to ensure that content is delivered consistently by the people who pick it up and run a course from it. They may not have time to prepare or to develop their own material, so you, the author, are doing their thinking for them. Every conceivable question might need to be anticipated and the content covered in enough depth that they can still inspire confidence in the audience. Equally, a team working on the same event will be singing from the same song sheet if they have all read the manual. Conversely, if you are running something that is leading to an accredited qualification such as NVQs, or a course that aims to standardize practices throughout a company, 'sticking to the book' is crucial.

To make this possible a manual has to be clear, succinct and unambiguous. Many seasoned trainers regard manuals as being idiots' guides, but this is rarely the case. Running a course does need some skill and sensitivity. Nearly all manuals will assume a basic grounding in training skills, such as discussion leading, facilitation, running feedback and making presentations.

Writing a manual isn't a task to be undertaken lightly. It takes much longer to write a manual than it does to run the course it describes!

If this hasn't put you off here is an outline to ensure your trainer notes cover the options.

1 Checklist of equipment and facilities
2 Handouts and slides lists
3 Timetable overview, session by session
4 For each session:

   • Objectives
   • Main learning points
   • Content
   • Process/structure of session

Manuals are just one approach to teaching other trainers how to run a course. Other options for ensuring everyone knows what to do include:

   • Briefings of the training team

- Sitting in at the back
- Developing trainers from course participants
- Video-recording the sessions

PREPARING PARTICIPANTS

Participants rarely come to a course with no idea of what is going to happen. Whether they have an accurate picture is another matter.

Participants may expect your in-house course to be similar in nature to their last experience. It may have been safety training or it may have been business strategy, but how can you ensure that they are adequately prepared for your course?

Firstly, how do they get their impressions of what is going to happen? Think about what stories they are likely to hear and from who they will get them. These include:

- Horror stores from outside about other courses
- Participants' own experiences of courses, good and bad
- Experiences of other colleagues on the same or similar courses
- Their own manager discussing the value of the course
- Contact with you when the course was being designed
- Pre-course work or introductory letter
- A personal meeting or telephone call from you

It doesn't take much analysis to see how much control you have over some of the sources of information and whether they accurately reflect your course. To ensure they get an accurate and favourable impression of a course, so that they are well disposed towards it, you need to actively 'manage' the information about it.

What information do participants need? Much of it is the same as a social event. Imagine you have been invited to a party. What would you want to know to feel totally at ease before you got there? It might depend on how much of a party animal you are! But for many people it would be nice to know:

- Who is going to be there?
- Why is it being held?
- Where is it going to be?
- How can you get there?
- What time does it start and finish?
- Is dress formal or casual?
- Who pays for the food and any refreshment!
- Are special diets catered for?
- If it's a long way from home, or runs for more than a day (if only!) will accommodation be available?
- If it is, are you expected to share with someone?

A major difference between a party and a course is that the course has a more complex purpose. As a result participants might need to be told if:

- there is any pre-course work
- they need to speak to their manager about the course
- they should consider their objectives
- the trainer will be contacting them to discuss their needs before the course

PREPARING THE VENUE

Finding a Venue

In-house courses can easily be run in an office if you have space, but you may need to consider off-site or residential accommodation if:

- participants are travelling from other distant offices
- days need to be long to fit in the material
- on-site learning may be too close to the office environment for participants to feel at ease
- participants need reflection time away from office

interruptions or free of the temptation to 'pop out to sort out a small problem'

If you have a regular company training centre then your worries are over, but many companies prefer to book accommodation as and when they need it. If this is the case, finding and booking a good venue will always add to your planning time and the lead time.

Conference venue-finding agencies can often smooth away much of the hassle. They work much like estate agents do for house buyers. A good agency should be able to identify suitable and available spaces in an area you define, negotiate rates, and arrange viewings for you. In the UK, agencies don't usually charge you, but get their fee from the hotel or conference centre. This means that you don't always get the lowest rates, but a good agency with good contacts should know what special deals are available.

Until you know a venue well don't assume that someone else's idea of a room that can take '30 people in comfort' is the same as yours! Neither is price a good indicator of quality – I've been offered converted hotel bedrooms for a course of 12 participants for the same price as another hotel's splendid oak-panelled boardroom.

For a good room for a course look for:

- Natural daylight, which can be excluded by curtains or blinds if you are using projection equipment.
- Enough space for participants to be able to move about the room freely, once the room has been laid out with your preferred seating plan.
- Comfortable seats (try them out and imagine sitting on them for three hours).
- Good ventilation and room temperature, ideally controllable from the room itself.

- Basic equipment like flip charts and overhead projectors provided free.
- A high enough ceiling for projection screens to be visible to all participants.
- Walls onto which you can post flip charts. Special flip chart rails are ideal, but otherwise a wallcovering that can take blu-tac or masking tape without damage. Beware the splendid ballroom decorated with flock wallpaper – it's very expensive to repair!

A good venue should also have:

- Separate areas to have lunch, tea and coffee breaks. This gives participants a change of scenery and avoids the distraction of tea being wheeled into the main room.
- Break-out, or syndicate, rooms of adequate size, also with natural daylight, capable of fitting in tables, flip charts and any other equipment.
- Water or fruit juices provided and refreshed during the day.
- An efficient message-taking service, with the messages passed over in the way you choose: either at breaks only, or passed into the room as they come in.

If your course is residential, a venue should be able to satisfy participants so that you and they can get on with learning without having to spend time on accommodation problems. The attitude of the reception staff and conference manager is often a good predictor of the level of service you can expect. Good service can often compensate for slightly less than adequate facilities, but most trainers will find that the best five-star accommodation can rarely compensate for bad or indifferent service. If lunch, tea or coffee arrives late, or if there isn't enough of it, it's a hassle you don't need. Equally, participants are giving up their own time for their employers and therefore usually expect something that is reasonably close to the level of comfort they might expect at home. Look for:

- Comfortable and clean en-suite bedrooms with working space and good lighting.
- Lounge areas where they can meet other participants, sit in comfort, and get refreshments.
- Menus that allow for special diets and variety from day to day. Longer courses feel even longer if there's no choice apart from the dreaded Black Forest gateau!
- Leisure facilities that help people relax. Long courses may prevent participants from doing their usual exercise routines (if they have them) but with good facilities they can unwind and recharge their batteries. Obviously it's no good having a splendid leisure club if your course allows no time to use it. If so it's better not to go to such a venue, or to give participants advance warning so that they can choose to arrive early and arrange to stay on if they want to use the facilities. You could also arrange for a hotel to allow early check-in, or get a special deal for participants who might want to stay an extra night.

Room Layouts
How you arrange a room communicates to participants the style of the course. Think about the method of teaching you are using, then choose the style you want reflected. Options include:

Lecture theatre with tables – good if a lot of writing is required, and presentations are being made from the front, or participants are equipped with computers for hands-on practice. Gives a formal atmosphere and leaves some people much further away from the trainer. For wide rooms tables can be laid out in herring-bone style so that no one has to turn their head all day to see a screen.

U-shape with tables – same advantages as a lecture theatre but takes more space. Enables everyone to be effectively in the front row – the trainer can walk up into the U and be near them all. Can also be arranged with an inner U and an outer U for larger groups. Less formal than lecture theatre but uncomfortable if a projector is being used a lot.

U-shape chairs, without tables – popular for courses where group discussion is used more and people may be asked to move around into groups in the main room. Disadvantage: inconvenient for writing notes or resting heavy manuals.

Cabaret style – participants are grouped around tables. Most informal table set-up, allowing trainers to wander most easily from table to table. Creates natural 'table syndicates' for buzz-groups and syndicate exercises. However, unless tables are large, most people end up at right angles or with their backs to a screen and have to twist round their chairs. If the room is large enough, place chairs only on one side of each table so that no one has to rotate right around.

Bean bags or cushions on floor (bring your own!) – for the most informal course of all, on a budget. Provides a relaxed setting for learner-centred courses. Easily rearranged layouts for exercises. Rarely comfortable for more than 15 minutes.

Trainer positions

The position of the trainer(s) creates an impression. Participants may infer how the trainers see their roles: facilitative, experts, learner-centred, assessors, and so on. Make sure your layout reflects your desired approach.

If participants have tables then trainers may decide to use a separate table, or put themselves on the same tables. When using a separate table, putting it at the front gives a formal conference impression and places the trainer as 'expert'. A table at the side is a more neutral position. This still allows any trainers not working to observe the group and their reactions. If a trainer 'chips in' to a debate then a side position is still acceptable – people don't need to crane their necks to see him/her. A table at the back is also neutral, though being out of view can be just as distracting as being at the side if seated trainers are talking, and chipping in is more awkward.

6

UNDERSTANDING DIFFERENT CULTURES

> *'Men's natures are alike – it is their habits that carry them far apart'*
>
> **Confucius**

Today's organizations are increasingly multinational, multi-cultural or both. Training needs to reflect this. Whether you are training in your own country with multinational participants, or you are training overseas with local participants, cross-cultural aspects will influence your effectiveness.

Trainers need to be aware of how different cultures can affect the way people see things, the way they communicate, and the way the trainer needs to act and speak to avoid misunderstandings.

This chapter looks at how:

- cultural differences can affect training situations
- you can become more aware of your own corporate and national culture
- you can plan your course to take local culture into account
- you can respond to cultural differences, be more clearly understood and can develop good rapport with participants from other cultures.

CULTURE AND TRAINING

We often judge people's behaviour against our own inter-pretation of what it means and why it happens. But in different cultures, behaviour is symptomatic of the under-lying values and beliefs a person holds.

For example, a participant arriving 20 minutes late for a course would be 'late' in the UK. In Arabic countries they would be 'on time'. This is because in the UK our underlying values and beliefs are those of the Protestant work ethic, and time costs money. But in Arabic countries, 'when Allah made time he made plenty of it'.

Geert Hofstede, when researching cultural differences arrived at four dimensions which he called:

- Power-Distance
- Individualist-Collectivist
- Masculinity (which includes its opposite, Femininity)
- Uncertainty Avoidance

As part of Hofstede's work he rated 40 countries on each scale. Some of the examples below illustrate the differences measured by Hofstede and how they can strike you when it comes to how people behave.

Training in the Far East

An example of the underlying differences of culture can be found in the difference between many Far Eastern countries and the UK or US. In the UK and US we have a predominantly individualistic culture. People grow up to take care of themselves and their immediate family, and have loyalty firstly to them, and then to their organization. In most Far Eastern countries the culture is collectivist. People are brought up in extended families to which they give their loyalty in return for protection. This concept of family is extended to the organizations they work for. It doesn't do to criticize the employing company in any way.

At the same time UK-US culture is predominantly low power-distance. Bosses and subordinates regard themselves as basically the same. Big differences in status are frowned upon. Many Far Eastern countries such as Singapore, Thailand and Hong Kong are higher power-distance.

Differences between boss and subordinate are accepted and the boss may well have status symbols, which are also accepted.

'Take me to your leader'

I noticed these differences when working in Brunei. The combination of collectivist culture and higher power-distance is demonstrated by respect for authority and elders. In groups participants often didn't speak for themselves but deferred to, and were spoken for by, their most senior member. If groups were more equal in seniority then they were more able to speak out. This also applied when I worked with Indonesian engineers in the UK.

'Where are the tables?'

Because of the high respect for authority, training is often lecture-style in the Far East. Participants expect to be addressed sitting at tables in a conference room. We had been told of this before we got there. Because our programmes were experiental and required movement and lots of quick group work in the main room, we decided to stick to our usual arrangement of no tables – just a U-shape of chairs. Nearly half the participants came in, shook our hands, then immediately said 'where are the tables?' Tables were a symptom of training culture. Our wish to train in a different way was important, but needed explaining. Once we had done so, people were happier about it.

Training in Eastern Europe

Behaviour can be explained by some of the long-standing teachings of a society. It is what helps people to interact smoothly. But sometimes it is driven by more recent political or economic influences:

'A participant is missing'

When running courses in Romania I found that participants often disappeared from a course, frequently with no warning. They would turn up later, mentioning 'a meeting' they had to attend. I found this strange, but only later discovered a possible reason for it. Romania still has a desperately poor economy by Western standards. Average annual earnings are not much more than US$1,500. As a result people are always looking out for cheap goods.

My local contact explained that people would cover for each other while they popped out of the office to join in a queue for something. If someone was called for while they were out of the building they were said to be 'visiting another department' or 'in the toilet' – sometimes for quite a time! But because this was an established way of dealing with the cost of living, management did not challenge the practice. A course was the perfect excuse to be absent from the office, and a meeting was the perfect excuse to be absent from the course!

This might not have been the real reason for the absences, but as a trainer I found it distressing. I couldn't keep track of participants and had sometimes only two-thirds of my full complement at any one time. My solution was to be flexible enough to re-integrate participants who had been away, and to help them to feel all right about their absences by not questioning them but merely asking them to give me warning so I could help them to rejoin later.

'Can you hear me . . . at the front?'
You can't always assume that training is given the same priority or funding outside your culture. I found that the rooms made available for training were very much removed from my normal experience. In the UK most of us expect a plush hotel, or a comfortable purpose-built conference centre. Training in most UK organizations has reasonable funding that means venues can be good for learning. It also means that people are lured away from their work by the promise of a good day with good food in a nice location.

My experience of Romanian venues was that equipment

was often not working and needed spare parts; room temperatures were in the 80s, as air conditioning was rare; and lighting was poor. One of the venues, a training centre, was next to a building site. We had the choice of frying with the windows closed, or being unable to hear ourselves speak with them open.

The participants were bright, highly educated, and had a good grasp of English. Although I was appalled at what they had to contend with, they were not surprised at the training conditions; they did not expect them to be better than their office.

'You cannot be serious!'

In Germany and parts of Eastern Europe participants usually expect trainers to be serious. Humour is not valued in business. A colleague who went out to train in Poland found his jokes were treated with surprise first of all, until the participants got used to the strange Englishman joking about serious subjects.

KNOWING YOUR OWN CULTURE

Often we are only aware of our own culture when we experience a clash with another one. But knowing something about your own culture can help you to avoid making assumptions that might create difficulties when running a course.

If you have run or attended programmes overseas you may have noticed some of the differences that existed between the cultures. Sometimes just attending courses in other companies can make you aware of your own culture.

To get a feel of some of the cultural values you take for granted in training, note down some answers to these questions:

Think back to the first course you attended in your current organi-

zation (or last, if you have not yet attended any).

- What things do you remember seeing, smelling, feeling?
- What did you do when you arrived?
- What did you find strange, comfortable, shocking or promising?
- Who did you identify with; why?
- Who did you see as different to you; why?
- Reflecting on your answers, what do they tell you about the culture of training on that course?

And for some of the cultural norms that other people also follow on your courses:

Think of a moment on the course when a rule was broken or disrupted.

- What happened?
- What was the result?
- What was the rule that was broken and how did it come to light?

What does this say about the rules, spoken and unspoken and the values that underlie them?

And for the trainers of the courses:

- Who are the 'best' trainers in your organization; why?
- Who are the 'worst' trainers; why?

What does this say about the organization's cultural values about who trains.

PREPARING YOURSELF FOR A COURSE IN A NEW CULTURE

Being able to work effectively in a different culture requires planning and responsiveness. This section covers the preparation tips that you can use before a course. The next section covers what you can do to respond to cultural differences.

Read, read, read
Books that give you local flavour can be very helpful, especially those which cover local customs, manners and culture. These can give useful pointers on general local issues.

Cultural briefings
Get a general briefing
If you are going overseas, speak to someone from the area beforehand. Ask them what is different about your own culture compared to theirs, and what you can do to get on well with theirs.

Get a training brief
A work group or manager can help to identify their learning culture by highlighting what makes them uncomfortable, when they are talked through the course design in detail. These areas of discomfort indicate that the learning culture is different from your assumption. You may need to probe about what is 'normal' for them. What would they expect to be done usually and why?

When I ran courses in the Far East I tapped into the learning culture before the course by discussing what was normal with the local training officer. The huge phone bill was well worthwhile because this identified a number of differences that I wouldn't have known about otherwise. Some of these differences and similarities include:

• The hours worked were fewer but the day started earlier.
• Friday lunch-times are long to allow for prayers.
• Role-play exercises are rarer so need a lot of positioning for their purpose and goal.

- Expatriate staff tended to dominate groups so were best placed together or with equally strong members of the local staff.
- Homework is difficult to do when participants return to their families.
- Role play using video camera is rare but not unknown so is acceptable.
- Direct feedback between participants is harder than it is in the UK especially between a younger participant and their elder because of the potential for loss of face, part of the Far Eastern culture.

Consider all of the details you have been given and compare them with your training design assumptions. What do you need to change to work better in that culture? What can stay the same but will need explaining because it is unknown? When will you have to behave differently to make things work?

Find a mentor

When you are in foreign territory, find a local person who can act as your cultural mentor, to help you interpret what is going on.

Inevitably the most wide-ranging briefing won't uncover every aspect of a learning culture. As trainers we have to be alert to signals about what is needed, and *adapt* our approach to them.

RESPONDING TO CULTURAL DIFFERENCES

Part of being sensitive to cross-cultural issues is being prepared to show you care and value the other person's culture as well as your own. Theirs is neither better, nor worse than your own, it is just a different way of doing things. Here are some tips gleaned from my own travels and those of others, not as a comprehensive list, but as examples of what you should be aware of.

Managing the first impressions you make

Show respect for local customs and language

The more of the local language you can learn, the more you will delight those with whom you are working. For short trips, at least *good morning* or *hello, goodbye*, and *thank you* will be rewarded with a smile.

Find out how people are addressed. Different people may use family names and first names in different ways, even in the same country, depending on religion. For example you might have had written communication from a Chinese man named Fred How Tok Kwan. Fred is usually the friendly name he would like to be addressed by face to face. 'How' is his family name. If you ring his switchboard they might not know Fred How, so use his full name. Whereas a letter signed Haji Abdul Rahim indicates that as a Muslim, the writer has made the pilgrimage to Mecca and should be given the respect of his title 'Haji'.

Names and titles vary from country to country. English names seem just as confusing to other nationalities as theirs are to us. Ask your local contact about the names, and be prepared to ask people how they should be addressed if you are still unsure. It is better to be respectful than presumptuous.

Don't make any assumptions

Different countries attach different meanings to the same word. In Japan 'Yes' means 'I am listening' not 'yes I agree'.

Different cultures attach different meanings to the same body language. In many parts of Asia, casting the eyes downwards when replying is a mark of respect, whereas in many Western countries it is regarded as a sign of duplicity.

Meal habits can vary widely. Lunch in England can be 45 minutes if you need to get through some material and want to cut corners. In France, you'll get raised eyebrows if it's that short. In Romania, people often don't have lunch at all, which can make you feel a bit awkward as you go off for a bite to eat.

Watch out for crossed communications

Notice the impact of your behaviour rather than its intent. It is very easy to insult someone even when your intention is the opposite. A trainer cracking a joke to dispel tension in one culture is being sensitive. In another they are being the opposite because they have caused someone to lose face by not treating them seriously.

Humour rarely travels; in-jokes never do

Different cultures have different attitudes to jokes. Britons like wordplay and sarcasm. Americans like visual humour. Germans don't want jokes at all at work; they feel it is not business-like.

Body language and contact

Different cultures have different ranges of intimate zones and rules for touching between sexes. For example, in Brunei it is not acceptable for a man to reach out and shake a Muslim woman's hand unless she offers hers first.

Equally, don't point with your index finger, use the thumb and motion to people with your hand palm-downwards as if you were scooping money off a table, rather than using a curled finger.

Learning how to work across cultures

Expect to feel uncomfortable with another culture

If you feel comfortable with another culture you may be imposing your own cultural values and not adapting to others. There are four common responses from people facing other cultures:

1   *'Ours is the only way'* – therefore anything which is dif-

ferent is not cultural, just the individual's strange behaviour.

2   *'Ours is the best way'* – which requires you only to acknowledge other cultures, understand why they are different but not to change anything you do.

3   *'Yours is the best way'* – which means you 'go native' when in another country and adopt all the behaviours that the locals do.

4   *'Ours is one way of many'* – which requires you to notice differences of approach and to look at how you can adapt your behaviour to make things work better.

When you feel uncomfortable, plan for action
As in the learning cycle outlined in chapter 4, feeling uncomfortable is feedback to yourself. For it to be useful in working in another culture you have to use it. The diagram below shows how it can become an invaluable tool.

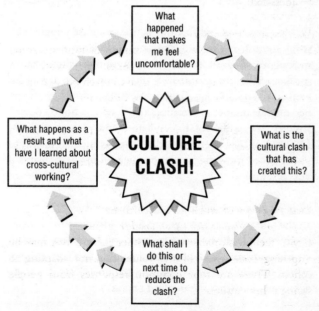

Learning to communicate across cultures

The moral is: don't ignore your own feelings, act on them.

Skills that help you bridge cultural gaps
Listen like you've never listened before
Work hard at actively listening – checking your understanding of what people have said by repeating things back to them.

Build trust by asking for feedback and listening to it. Offer feedback in return without judging the person.

When people are not using their mother tongue, listen for the meaning behind what they are saying rather than the words they use. Although English is the international business language, it carries far too many words for most to use as a fine tool. Many languages have only one word for something when English has several variations.

Communicate clearly
Double negatives and fine distinctions confuse people who speak English as a second language, as do jargon words and metaphors. English is full of such things which native speakers take for granted. I once remember trying to explain to some Indonesian engineers the phrase 'getting a bee in your bonnet' by relating it to 'having a hobby horse'! Instead, use words of one syllable, and plenty of them. Other languages often depend on explaining the context to give a word meaning. It is more helpful for participants if you do this too.

Help people understand you and what you are doing
In the same way as you need to listen for meaning, it helps to give people the meaning to what you are doing. Explain clearly your goals and what you are doing to achieve them. When outlining exercises, explain the goal, how it is to be achieved, and what the method entails.

Remember how long it takes you to read something in

another language. Give participants longer for preparation and try to keep briefing notes short. Use pictures to explain how exercises work. Ask open questions to check for understanding.

7

DESIGNING A COURSE SESSION

Designing sessions is often the most creative part of running a course. Creativity is important so that participants:

- See how learning something is useful for them
- Are motivated by stimulating approaches
- Achieve their learning in different ways
- Have learning points reinforced, without being patronized

If you are really creative you probably won't need to read this section, but if like 95 per cent of people you'd rather not reinvent the wheel, then you can use the list of methods given in this chapter for some ideas. You can give them your creative 'spin' to make them fit well with your learning objectives and the organization.

This chapter covers three aspects of design:

- The main components a learning design should include
- The methods available
- Completing a design

WHAT SHOULD A LEARNING DESIGN INCLUDE?
A good frame of mind to be in is one that is caring and fun. I was once told a neat way of thinking about designing a session: imagine you are just about to teach a child or a friend. How would you go about it?

A basic learning design includes the following parts:

1   Motivate the learner to learn – what's in it for me?
2   Outline what is to be learned and how the learning method works, and link to previous and future sessions

of the course.

3   Input the learning points – exercise, lecture, etc.
4   Review the learning points and check understanding
5   Action plan – how will you use this in real life?

How detailed you are with these stages depends on the session design. For instance, a role-play to discover different approaches for calming down an irate customer is not going to be preceded by telling the participants what the techniques are! This is discovery learning, so what is needed is an overview of how the learning method works and what is expected of the participants – to experiment and try different approaches. The content is then reviewed at the end and will be summarized later.

This is in contrast to the traditional lecture or presentation in which we are usually instructed to: 'Tell them what you are going to tell them; tell them; then tell them what you told them.'

With any technique you use, think how you are going to integrate the five parts of the learning design. You can remember it using the acronym **MOIRA**:

Motivate
Overview
Input
Review
Action

METHODS FOR LEARNING

The rest of this chapter covers the range of methods you have available. Some needs lots of time; others need lots of trainers, space, materials, or participants to make them work. Be well aware of your own limitations. If you are new to training it is better to go with a technique that you understand and can make fun, than to pick something you've never seen or experienced and then watch it go wrong.

Action learning

This term can be taken as anything involving physical action to enliven learning, like having to perform a song or to act out an aspect of what is being learned. In other circles, action learning, or action-learning sets involve small groups of participants applying learning to their work, problem-solving, or carrying out projects either individually or in teams which reinforce skills. Both interpretations have the same principle: that to do something is more powerful than to see it, hear it or talk about it.

Before and after tools

Testing the skills or knowledge of participants before and after a course can be an invaluable way of evaluating its effectiveness. But even if you don't want to do tests you can use this as a way of giving participants the satisfaction of measuring their progress. You can either set questions beforehand and use the same ones afterwards (or after each session), or get participants to pose their own questions, to which they don't know the answers, and then give them the satisfaction of being able to answer them later.

Brainstorming

A group often has the answers if it looks deep enough and thinks laterally enough. The trainer gets the group to call out answers to a well-phrased problem as either: 'How to . . . calm down an irate customer' or 'Ways of . . . developing more business'. It is important to define the problem first. Then make sure some simple rules are followed:

- Go for quantity ('Let's fill up 3 flip charts in 5 minutes')
- Don't evaluate ideas until the end (No 'Yes buts')
- Build on ideas where possible ('Yes and . . . ')
- Don't be inhibited from coming up with ideas

BUZZ GROUPS

The name comes from the 'buzz' of small groups working together on a problem. Buzz groups are useful for creating energy in a group. It also helps draw out ideas when asking a whole group or individuals may result in nobody replying. Make small teams of 3-5 people, grouped as they are sitting, and give them a few minutes to come up with ideas, comments or suggestions, which a spokesperson then calls out. Avoid moving people around the room or out of the room as this takes too much time.

Case study
A written, video-recorded or story-told example of a real-life or imaginary situation or incident. After taking in the information, participants may be asked to define a problem and to come up with recommendations for what should be done. The method is useful for applying learnt skills of diagnosis, analysis, problem solving and identifying solutions.

Checklists
Checklists can act as a prompt after a course until new skills become automatic, or to help in situations which happen only occasionally when the skills can be remembered with prompting. You can also ask participants to devise their own checklists, individually or in groups. This acts as both a learning review and the reinforcement tool. Encourage them to create personal checklists in the style they prefer: linear lists, pictures or mind-maps.

Coaching
Coaching can range from providing feedback to an individual on parts of a learnt skill so that they can improve it; to helping them to understand a problem and create a solution to it. The interpretations of coaching merge into counselling so the two have been separated here by their focus: coaching is an *external* focus, such as problems or skills; counselling has an *internal* focus, including blocks due to clashes with values or self-beliefs.

A coaching session can take an individual through a problem-solving process by asking the right questions:

- *Problem questions* – 'What is the problem right now?'
- *Option questions* – 'What different ways might you overcome this?'
- *Solution questions* – 'Which is your preferred solution?' or 'Which one could you try first?'
- *Action questions* – 'What are the steps to achieving this?'

Counselling to overcome blocks

Participants may encounter internal blocks to learning new skills or knowledge. These blocks are sometimes known as 'self-talk', 'vicious and virtuous circles' and 'self-fulfilling prophecies'. An example is shown below.

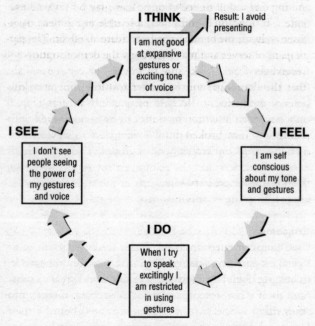

Example of a negative block when making a presentation

Counselling involves helping the participant to identify the personal block which prevents them from effective performance. The next step is to 'bust the block' by breaking into the cycle. This can be done in different ways:

- *Positive reinforcement* – making the person change their belief about their ability.
- *Coaching and practice* – to improve the skill itself.
- *Positive feedback* – by getting the person to focus on what is good rather than what is bad.
- *Relaxation* – to overcome self-consciousness and stress which undermine good performance.
- *Creating a supportive climate* – ensuring that the participant has low-risk situations in which to practice, also reducing stress.

Demonstration

Acting out a skill or technique. This may be how to execute a routine on a computer, assemble equipment, stand assertively, or use certain words to create an effect. The participant observes and may then copy the demonstration and receive feedback. Make sure that everyone can see and also that the demonstration is neither too long nor at a low-energy time of day. Because participants are not directly involved their attention span may be short. Complex operations are best broken into several demonstrations with practice of each part.

Diagnostic questionnaires

A questionnaire or survey instrument, usually paper-based, that gets participants to evaluate their own skill or knowledge level. This may be by asking them to evaluate a case study, answer questions based on the course content, or get feedback on their skills or behaviour from colleagues and manager. Useful for motivating participants before a course, and also for pinpointing particular difficulties or weak areas they may have.

To be effective, the questionnaire should be tested out on a small sample first. This ensures that questions are not confusing and that the results are as expected.

Discussion

Involves participants more than a lecture does and helps us to uncover knowledge and attitudes about a subject. It may be preceded by a lecture followed by some open questions to prompt discussion from the group. Further questions act to guide it.

The trainer can act as a facilitator by encouraging participants to address the rest of the group, or the trainer can remain the focus of the discussion if he or she has a great deal of subject knowledge. The trainer ensures that everyone has the opportunity to speak and that individuals are not allowed to dominate. The content may be recorded on a flip chart, or the trainer may restate and summarize participants' points.

Energizers

An energizer activity serves to stimulate participants when they are feeling fatigued, to break up a series of sessions which have no physical movement, or as a wake-up. Energizers may involve physical or mental activity and are often used first thing in the morning or after lunch, in the 'graveyard slot'.

Possible activities depend on space available and the acceptability of 'silly games' with a group – many children's games can be adapted. Possibilities include: stretch to sky, shake tension out of arms and legs, ball catching, relay races, musical chairs. More staid options include: brain-teasers, 5-minute stretch breaks, or a walk about.

Exercise

An exercise is a task given to solve a problem. It is often pen and paper based, but can be a hands-on exercise, like solving a problem on a printed circuit board, or being asked to execute a task on a new piece of software. The problem focuses on a specific learning point and usually has one correct answer.

A series of problems can be given, which may become progressively harder. The trainer can leave it up to participants to seek help or can go round to check on progress and make corrections as necessary.

Reviewing an exercise ensures that everyone has been able to find the correct answer and how to get to it. Difficulties can be discussed. An exercise can also be scored and used as a test.

Feedback

Feedback allows participants to review what they have done from another person's perspective. It is useful for understanding the impact of their actions and the way they communicate. Feedback can be from other participants or a trainer. It can be done in conjunction with video recording to provide a second view. For participants unused to feedback or threatened by past feedback which has been hurtful, it can help to agree guidelines with them. Good feedback needs to be:

- *Specific* – say exactly what happened e.g. 'you leaned forward' rather than 'you looked dominating'.
- *Changeable* – about behaviour – which can be changed – rather than about someone's characteristics.
- *Neutral in description* – avoid evaluative words such as 'domineering' which result in the receiver wanting to defend their action.
- *A gift* – given for the receiver's benefit, not the giver's.
- *Clarified* – encourage questions so the receiver understands.
- *Timely* – given soon after the event so the receiver can still recall it.
- *About positive and negative* – reinforce the good as well as saying which things need to be changed. I sometimes ask for 'things to do differently' and 'things to stay the same'.
- *Owned by the giver* – this is achieved by describing the

impact using 'I' rather than 'we' or 'one', e.g. 'I felt threatened by this'.

Giving good feedback isn't easy. Be prepared to give guidance by asking clarifying questions when a participant is trying to provide feedback to another. And step in when things are going wrong. If the participants have already heard the guidelines it is easier to get them back on track.

Equally, to prepare people for receiving feedback, tell them:

- *It is just useful data* – to be evaluated and then either acted on or rejected. The first impact of feedback may be surprise or shock, sometimes leading to anger and rejection of it. Encourage people to sleep on it and decide the next day whether it is valid.
- *To clarify what they don't understand* – ask questions to make it more specific, understand the impact etc.
- Not to argue or explain – the event is past. Feedback is for future use. It is not a review of why something was done.

Fishbowl
A technique to enable participants to be aware of process, or different aspects of process; or to engage in a controlled discussion. The name stems from the way one group is arranged around another, observing them as if the inner group were in a fishbowl. The inner group is engaged in an activity, like a discussion or decision about how to solve a problem. The outer group is arranged in a circle around the inner group and watch the process of the activity.

Process variation – Usually one or more of the outer group is allocated to observe someone in the inner group. Alternatively, members of the outer group may be asked to look for different types of behaviour. The exercise can thus be used to give feedback to the inner members (without their observers having to engage in the action), or to give the observers practice in classifying behaviour. When reviewing a fishbowl, the outer members can give feedback to their corresponding inner member. Alternatively, the trainer asks the observers to first review what happened within their team, and then to compare the different roles played.

Discussion variation – this enables a controlled discussion to go on in the inner circle with the outer circle observing. The inner circle may comprise four or five experts, or selected members of the group. Outer circle members can act as advisers to their opposite members inside, or can replace them in the conversation after a pre-arranged signal such as a tap on the shoulder. The discussion then continues, like tag wrestling.

Games or competitions

Games or competitions create energy to be focused on a task because they are fun. Games can create memorable situations. They call on the inventiveness of the trainer to make up questions or to create a framework which allows the participants to practise skills, such as teamwork, in a competitive environment. Adaptations of popular TV game shows or party games mean that participants understand more easily how they are run and scored.

Competitions need a simple scoring system which gives a measure of success so that participants can then move their attention fully on to reviewing the activity's process rather than its content.

Short games are better – a game or competition which is too long may result in poor recollection of what happened from participants. This can be partly overcome by midway reviews and trainers observing and taking notes.

Handouts

Covers any written documents that help a participant's understanding of either the content of a course, or its process. For example, they can be given a note of the main steps in a diagnostic process, then be asked to apply it. Alternatively, an exercise or role-play may have a written brief to outline the steps involved.

Handouts should be as short as possible so that participants can read them quickly. Variations in reading speed, especially with non-native language speakers, are then not so noticeable. Alternatively, give out handouts before a break or to be read overnight.

Incident report

Similar to a case study, an incident report involves the trainer telling participants some details of an incident. The details are incomplete so that participants have to ask questions to fill in the gaps. Using this method, participants learn to gather information about events leading up to an incident and to evaluate it.

A well-told incident report can be stimulating and has more reality than a written case study. The easiest method to construct an incident report is for the trainer to have been involved in the genuine incident on which it is based. If it is fictional then considerable planning is required so that the trainer can give out the information without needing notes and can be consistent and accurate.

In-tray

An in-tray comprises written materials representing a series of tasks and incidents which a manger's role might encompass on a 'typical' day' – or perhaps a 'worst day' might be more precise. The participants have to prioritize the actions required and indicate how they would respond. More sophisticated in-tray exercises might then ask them to perform the required tasks, depending on what they decide to do.

The exercise can be done individually or as a group, though the latter would test different abilities because a group can multi-task but needs co-ordination.

In-trays have a number of benefits: they have good 'face validity' (i.e. they reflect real life so training appears directly relevant), they can be a good test of priority judgement and of time management. For these reasons they are most often used in assessment or development centres where ability to perform whole jobs is measured, rather than individual skills.

A tailor-made in-tray takes a great deal of time to prepare, both to create the scenarios, the supporting materials, and the expert answer which participants like to measure their performance against. The exercise needs to be carefully reviewed afterwards for learning points.

Interview
An interview involves one person acting as interviewee while a group or one person acts as interviewer. The interviewee is chosen as an expert in their field or as someone whose views will be of interest; for example a senior manager.

The technique is interesting to both interviewee and interviewers. The interviewee does not have to prepare anything. The interviewers ask the things they are most interested in, and can pursue topics in greater depth. The trainer may have to:

- Keep discussion on track to avoid wandering away from the main topic
- Prevent anyone from dominating the discussion, including the interviewee

- Prompt questions by sowing some beforehand or through buzz groups
- Inform the interviewee in advance of any questions that might need research.

Lecture, input or presentation

Lectures involve presenting facts, concepts and models orally to a group. They are often supported by visual aids. Lectures can last up to 40 minutes; the term input has been coined for shorter sessions of 5-10 minutes.

By their nature, lectures do not actively involve participants. To allow for involvement they are often coupled with buzz groups, discussion etc.

Lectures are a good way of ensuring that everyone receives the same message. To ensure the good attention of participants the presenter has to be skilled and well prepared. Attention span dwindles over time, so shorter sessions are better. Failing that, break up a session by some interaction to refresh.

For very big groups, lectures are one of the few methods available. Make sure that everyone can see and hear it. To achieve this, consider amplifying your voice and using large screen projection.

Mind-maps

These are a helpful way of enabling participants to remember key issues and linkages of ideas. Constructing a mind-map is covered on page 40. Mind-maps can be provided as pre-printed pages of notes, built up on blackboards or flip charts as a lecture progresses, or can be taught to participants beforehand as a learning aid.

Mnemonics

Memory devices which help recall include acronyms and rhymes. Many people can still remember the spectrum through 'Richard of York gave battle in vain'. Appraisal objective-setting is recalled by SMART (Specific, Measurable, Achievable, Realistic, Time-framed) and strategic business analysis is helped by SWOT (Strengths, Weaknesses, Opportunities, Threats).

Helping participants to remember doesn't always require a trainer to have the vocabulary of a lexicographer! Many participants can just as ably come up with a good mnemonic as a game, and in so doing, remember even better.

Modelling of behaviours or skills

When participants need to learn a new behaviour or skill they often find it useful to see what it should look like. A trainer can help by showing how it is done, both in class and in other situations – working with participants, during evening meals etc. It is important to let participants know that you are modelling the behaviour. The action can be overdone or done realistically, but the participants need to know which it is, as an overdone model appears ridiculous and puts people off if it isn't recognized as such.

Modelling doesn't have to be performed perfectly either. This can give participants the opportunity to identify ways in which it can be improved. This encourages them to break the action down further so they can diagnose difficulties in performance and make corrections.

Another use of modelling is to make participants sensitive to a particular behaviour so they can identify it and give feedback to others who are also trying to use it.

Modelling can be done live, trainer to participants; between trainers as a skit; and pre-recorded on video.

Panel discussion

A panel discussion usually involves between two and five experts or senior personnel who have prepared ideas in reply to questions or about a topic. The more people on the panel, the longer the discussion will take. The discussion is made in front of participants who then have an opportunity to ask questions. The trainer facilitates the process, ensuring equal air time for participants and panel members, sowing or prompting questions, and managing the discussion itself to keep it on track.

Like a lecture, panels often don't involve participants and some may withdraw or switch off. The trainer needs to be sensitive to those withdrawing and re-involve them. Again, longer discussions result in diminished attention from participants, so you need to break it up by other techniques which change the pace, structure or level of participation.

A panel can be useful when there may be different views on a subject. The purpose of the session can be to demonstrate the diversity of views, to encourage participants to respect the diversity, or to make a judgement based on the expert opinions.

Questioning

Questioning can be used in many different ways: to enable participants to get their own questions answered; to act as a review of learning; to allow those with more knowledge to help others; or a combination of all these. Here are some different ways of using them:

Question cards – The trainer writes or types a number of questions relating to the course content on to cards. Hand them out to participants and ask them to circulate until they find someone to answer the question.

One-on-one questions – Ask participants to write down their own questions then to pair up and ask the question of their partner.

Ask the wizard – Give participants post-it notes and ask

them to write down any questions they have which haven't yet been answered or that they would like to ask but haven't had an appropriate moment. Draw up a flip chart or white board with a picture of a wizard. Ask participants to stick their post-it notes on to the wizard to be answered later. Pass out the notes to other participants either singly or in groups and ask them to answer them fully, with a presentation if necessary. The trainer can help the groups or answer the questions directly if necessary.

Pass the hat – Each participant writes a question and drops it into the hat. It is then passed round again, everyone takes a card and has 30 seconds to answer it. Participants can be allowed to confer, or not.

Pub quiz/team quiz – Each participant is asked to think up three questions which are tricky, but should be capable of being answered from what has been covered. Three questions allow for overlap so most participants have some in reserve if someone else asks the same one. They ask the question of the group (to keep them all on their toes) then name the participant they want to answer it. The same game can be played in teams to allow some conferring and pooling of questions.

Role play

Role play involves two or more people taking on roles to act out a situation. The situation can be a few minutes or extended into hours. The roles can be quite dissimilar to the person's everyday role, or a participant may play themselves interacting with another participant. The value of role play is that it is a chance to try or observe the impact of behaviour without the risk that would be attached the real situation outside of the course.

A role-play can be used for:

- Diagnosis of behavioural patterns or difficulties in a

given situation

- Rehearsal of a real-life event, such as a meeting, enabling experimentation and practising of various tactics.
- Problem solving by other participants or trainers who gain a better understanding of a situation and can offer solutions.
- Understanding others' views by participants reversing roles with either another participant, or by adopting the role of someone outside of the course with whom they normally work.

Roles can be written by trainers or by participants. The level of detail required depends on the learning goals and the familiarity the various role players may have with the situation. Typical components of a role brief include:

- Situation, and known knowledge, including that known about other roles
- Characteristics and motivations of the role
- Objectives for the role

Participants need to know what the learning objectives are. Observers may need briefing for what to look for if they are drawn from the participants. The role play can also be video recorded for later review.

For maximum effect, role-play briefs often need to be tailored to the participants' experience. This gives face validity to the exercise and makes it easier to do, since less preparation is needed. The closer to real life that a role-play is, the less likely it is that a participant will claim that they 'wouldn't do it like that normally'. For this reason, although it takes more time, it often pays to ask participants to write their own role briefs for a situation.

Simulation
Simulations are realistic enactments of events, which give participants the chance to respond and see the conse-

quences of their actions. A simulation may be of a system, such as a chemical plant control room, a flight simulator, a business economics situation, an outdoor search and rescue mission, or leading a management team.

The component interacting with the participants may be a computer, a mock-up control room, or a group of actors. In the latter case, the main differences between a role-play and a simulation is that a simulation has a greater complexity and ability to interact with participants, is more realistic, and has more controlled outcomes.

Simulations tend to be costly to produce and run, depending on the level of technology required. However, when well run they have an extremely high level of acceptance among participants. The realism created by a good simulation can provoke the same emotions in a participant that the real-life situation would provoke, without the same cost to life, equipment or pride.

A technology-driven simulation needs to be carefully analyzed for the numerous decisions on a system and their likely impact. Each decision has an outcome which then opens a different range of possible decisions and outcomes. This results in a complex decision tree which needs to be programmed.

A people-driven simulation equally needs to consider the possible actions that participants may take and the likely outcomes, with the added complexity of different people responding in different ways to the same action. To be coherent, a simulator/actor needs to respond in the way that their character would respond. In longer simulations, participants can have the opportunity of stopping the action or back-tracking so that they can try other approaches, rather than compounding an error.

Skit

A skit is a short play, which a small group of participants usually produce in front of other group members. It is often given to participants to prepare in order to demonstrate a learning point. The trainer may give them additional material to build into the skit.

The learning points in skits may be from:

- the content (e.g. a skit about how *not* to welcome a customer), *or*
- the process of creating the skit (e.g. how to co-ordinate a team during problem solving and planning).

Too much planning time results in boredom. Reducing preparation time raises the participants' energy. For this reason, the learning points can be limited since the skit may be flawed. However, as a fun activity, from which a number of serious points can be extracted, it can be useful.

Syndicate groups

Syndicate, break-out or work groups are used so that participants can get into small teams to discuss issues, prepare ideas about a topic, or talk about their learning. The activity usually takes a minimum of 20 minutes and can be done in a corner of a large main room or, more usually, in separate, small syndicate rooms. When syndicate rooms are used it is important to allow time to get to and from the rooms and to ensure that they are reasonably close to the main room.

Syndicate groups can have a finite life, for example to discuss a topic and prepare a presentation to make to the main group. Or a syndicate can have a longer life over the span of a course, and can act as 'home' group at intervals. Participants can discuss their hopes and fears, their difficulties, and to get help from their fellow syndicate members.

For equipment, syndicate groups might need a table and

chairs, a flip chart and pens, and possibly acetates and pens. Check that everything is in place and the door is unlocked before the groups go to their rooms.

I have occasionally found a group to be perfectly clear about what they *thought* I said, but sometimes to be doing the opposite of what I *actually* said! This sometimes happens when a dominant syndicate member mishears, then convinces the rest that he or she is right. On very rare occasions it can also be due to poor briefing!

Don't assume that everyone is listening to your every word. It is often helpful to pop in at the beginning of a syndicate session to check that the group is clear, and is doing what you expected. Trainers can be present in syndicate meetings or can absent themselves.

Depending on the national and company culture the syndicate groups may come back dutifully on time, or may regard a deadline as purely a guide. Check that groups are reaching their conclusions at similar points. If they have never done this before, suggest how they could achieve the deadline. If you have never done the exercise before, and have perhaps underestimated the time, decide on whether you can allow an overrun. If so, tell all the groups what the new deadline is so that none are hanging around while the others continue.

Choosing teams
Members of groups for exercises and syndicate work may be determined by either the learning objective, which can be planned for; or to allow learning within a certain group. The groups may not be planned until the individuals are known. Factors include:

- Dominance and quietness – group all dominant people together or mix types
- Level of experience of a topic or of the method of achieving a task

- Other characteristics such as age, ethnic origin and sex
- Cliques of old friends – some cliques are too cosy and perform badly but other cliques perform very well. This may be because despite knowing each other, the participants care for each others' learning and they continue to help and challenge each other.
- Similar or complementary learning goals – this needs everyone to be aware of everyone else's goals. Flip charts on a wall can help this.
- Random choice to encourage participants to be flexible. A simple method is to number people off in the group as they are sitting: 1, 2, 3, 1, 2, 3 etc.
- Participants choose their own groups – this can be easier than the trainer having to work out a mix. However, during the dependent phase of a course, participants often don't like having to choose. It means they also have to choose who *not* to work with.

Video tapes

As a way of imparting learning points, or situations and possible responses, videos are widely recognized. They are controlled and repeatable, time after time. The initial cost of buying a generic video is moderately high, but after several uses the per-participant cost falls rapidly. The cost of producing an in-house video is much higher although production costs have fallen dramatically in recent years due to streamlined editing techniques and falling equipment costs.

Generic videos range from recordings of public lectures from well-known experts, to dramatize events which show physical disasters or management situations. Participants are getting increasingly sophisticated in their tastes because of higher than ever television standards. A badly-produced video, or an outdated one, can be worse than none at all.

Many generic video production houses have preview facilities to help in the selection process. There are also some training 'libraries' that offer videos from a range of suppliers, providing a one-stop shop. They make their money either by charging you for their preview facilities, or by processing your order and making a margin on the cost of the video in the same way that a shop would.

Higher priced videos can often be hired for a few days, when purchase for one-off use may be too expensive. Some of the video companies also provide accompanying booklets for participants, and for trainers. Trainer guides may give an outline of how the video can be used in a session, whether it can be broken up by exercises, and sometimes what exercises can be used.

COMPLETING THE DESIGN

After deciding on the methods to use for any sessions, plan for how long each will last and fit them into the overall time you have been given. Check that the learning points have a logical flow.

Debug the sessions by running through them with other members of the training team, a colleague, consultant or yourself. Debugging involves asking the questions:

- Does the method contribute to the learning goal?
- Is it clear what the method is?
- Are the method and content pitched at the right level?
- Can anything else go wrong?

A 'no' to any of these doesn't always mean you've got the wrong method. It might be that you need to polish it up to simplify it, add complexity, create clear instructions or plan some alternative methods.

After the methods, comes the preparation of notes and trainer guides, covered in the previous chapter.

Then comes the big day! The next chapter covers what you can do to make the perfect session.

8

RUNNING A SESSION

If you've already planned your session well, running it means executing it in the best way possible, and ensuring that you can respond to the group's and the individual's needs. This section therefore concentrates on the way you deliver your plan and tackles some of the nightmares that any trainer can encounter.

WHAT MAKES A GOOD TRAINER?

A good performance won't cover up lousy preparation, but a bad performance can spoil all those hours you put in beforehand. Participants don't get to see all the preparation you have done for the course. They may be impressed by the nice handouts, the neat activities you planned, and the splendid venue you found. But on the day, a lot of their judgement is swayed by you and any other trainers, and *how* you deliver the training.

Developing a model of best practice

Think about the difference between a good trainer's performance you have seen, and a bad one. What did they do? Include the elements of presentation, but also what the trainer did – from the moment they first met you on the course, the times they were working with you in small groups, and the moments when they chatted to you in breaks.

This may give you some of the inspirational models for your own training style. The space below gives you some prompts for different training stages. There's a blanket section for any other ideas which you have noticed at other times. List them here or on a separate sheet.

	What the best trainer I met did was . . .	What the worst trainer I met did was . . .
Welcoming		
Overviewing the course		
Presenting materials		
Working with small groups		
Working one-to-one		
Out of hours (breaks, meals)		

TIPS FOR THE NEW, REMINDERS FOR THE WEARY

In addition to your own tips which you've drawn from your model trainer, here are some other ideas for running a successful session.

Reinforce points in different ways, not by banging on about them

Presentations allow for some repetition in the opening and conclusion, but also reinforce points using stories, examples and handouts.

Be positive, not cynical

Avoid the temptation of showing your worldliness through cynicism. If nothing can be done, why train anyone?

Keep up your own energy, as well as participants'

By making sure you are well rested and relaxed you have the energy to inject it into a group. If you arrive exhausted or party in the bar longer than anyone else, you won't be in any fit state to re-energize any jaded souls the following day.

You don't have to stay up to watch over everyone. If it's a several-day course, take turns with the other trainers to enjoy the party. Otherwise have an early night. If you normally have an exercise routine and eat healthily, give yourself some space to keep it up on the course.

Signpost like mad

At the beginning of each session, tell participants how it will run. Telling participants about the links back and forward helps them to understand your logic, remember the points and feel reassured about what is to come.

Enjoy yourself

Hard to do, but if you have an attitude of 'I'm going to enjoy this course and the participants' then you'll get them relaxed and they'll enjoy it too. Go in with an attitude of 'this has to be done, and I'm the best one for the job' and the atmosphere will be worthy, serious and dull.

Know your participants

Everyone likes to be remembered. If you have difficulty remembering names, write them down during the introductions, use name tents on desks, get people to wear badges, and use their names when you first address them. Keep reminding yourself until you can relate the name to the face without looking at the name-plate. There are also some useful memory techniques in Tony Buzan's book *Speed Memory*

It's OK for people to feel weary, but not for you to ignore it

Watch out for signs of wandering attention. It may be eyes closing, slumping, heads resting on hands, drifting eyes, or questions repeated which have already been answered. Act!

- Move around and closer to those looking dozy
- Change the tone of your voice
- Try talking softer then louder
- Get the group active by changing the method
- Taking a stretch break
- Get the group to do a physical stretch in class

Everyone learns, even you

Encourage participants to regard everything as a learning opportunity by showing them that you do, too. Ask them for feedback and demonstrate openness to it. Welcome it, even the criticisms. Ask for feedback from your fellow trainers, and tell them beforehand if you are trying to develop anything in particular.

USING A TOOLKIT OF BEHAVIOURS

Because there are so many different methods you may be using, it helps to have a 'universal toolkit'. This is the range of interventions you use to execute your plan and to respond to what happens moment to moment. There are plenty of different models of behaviour. The one outlined below is specifically for a training and facilitation context.

You may like to think of your behaviours when they are directed to participants as 'interventions'. This is because they intervene in an ongoing process, for example a participant who is talking about their job. When you ask them a question, or suggest they tell you what is the key part of the job, you are intervening.

Having a framework for your interventions helps you to evaluate what you have done and its effectiveness. Feedback from co-trainers is also an important part of developing your judgement about what interventions you might use.

So if a colleague who gives you feedback can use the same framework for observing your behaviour, then you can quickly identify the appropriateness of what you have done and the way you did it.

A MODEL OF TRAINER INTERVENTIONS

At its basic level your style can be categorized as either 'Push' or 'Pull'. These two categories each cover three intervention styles:

Push
- Prescribing solutions or methods
- Challenging behaviour or views
- Giving information about content or process

Pull
- Asking questions
- Giving support
- Releasing tension

Push

Push styles are aimed mostly at taking responsibility for

learning from the participants. For example, it may be to give them information, offer answers to their work problems, tell them what they should be doing next in a course, or point out that they are not behaving according to the learning agreement. The trainer delivers their push style intervention *caringly* for the participant – imagine them as a good friend when you do it.

Pull

Pull styles aim to help participants to get into a better position to learn for themselves. For example, by asking questions which help them clarify what they think or know, by offering support by affirming their value and ability, or to help them release their tension by talking about something, relieving it, or by cracking a joke.

Appropriateness

The type of intervention style you will draw on depends on the overall style of course, as covered in the section on your approach to training (see Chapter 4). An instructor-led course is going to draw on more push styles, whereas a facilitator-led course will use more pull styles. Neither style is wrong, but it needs to be appropriate for the approach and the moment. In making an intervention, your appropriateness and effectiveness also depend on:

- Timing
- Content – the words that are used
- Manner – the body language, power and tone of your voice, eye contact

As you get feedback from your colleagues you can develop your skills of judgement and delivery. You will say the right thing at the right time in the right way. You'll become the perfect trainer.

WHAT GIVES TRAINERS NIGHTMARES?

Again, despite the best design, some things can go awry.

For some trainers, these are the nightmares of running courses; for others they are the challenges to be met. Most nightmares, though not desirable, can be planned for.

Here are some of the 'worst nightmares' mentioned on training courses I have run, with possible solutions to them.

'Call yourself a trainer, you can't answer my simple question!'

This embarrasses some trainers because they feel it makes them look ignorant or not sufficiently prepared. However, questions suggest that someone is interested. So encourage them, even if they are outside of your field of knowledge. Here are some possible strategies for question handling.

- Firstly, acknowledge it as an 'interesting' or 'good' question – one you don't know the answer to 'off-hand'.
- Ask the group what they think. If the question is really hard, form them into buzz groups to consider possibilities.
- Admit you don't know but find out the answer and feed it back. Or give the participant reference materials, ask them to look it up, and tell the rest of the group when they find it.
- Refer them to outside sources of help: books, a more advanced course, an expert you know in the company.
- If neither time nor resources are available, promise you will find out and let him/her know after the course. Make sure you do so.

'Sorry, I have to go before the end . . .'

The seriousness of participants leaving depends on whether they leave for a reason external to the course, or because of the course itself. The problem with early departures is three-fold: it signals lack of commitment to other members, it may leave a syndicate short of a team member, and the leaver misses out on part of the programme. They usually miss out even more than anticipated because their minds start wandering onto their journey or meeting well before they leave.

- I usually check at the outset of a course whether anyone may have to leave before the scheduled finishing time. That makes it harder for people to come up with excuses later about meetings. It also enables you to negotiate with the individual and the group about departure times.
- If the departure is only a little while before the end, try to negotiate shorter breaks so everyone can finish early.
- If the departure is very early suggest supportively that they could leave now and come back on another course when they can make the whole thing as they 'won't achieve the objectives from only half a course'. This gentle confronting may be enough to keep them committed and the 'urgent' need for their presence elsewhere may disappear.
- If they genuinely have to go either before the end, or for a short while in the middle of the course, offer to help them catch up, give them reading to do on their journey, give them the best time to go, and help them extract themselves gracefully from whatever group they may be working with.

'Oh no, where are the materials?'
This only happens when you are running a course miles from the office, and you look for your box of materials at 8.30 in the morning. Couriers do sometimes deliver late; hotels sometimes lose boxes (which turn up at the end of the course). It happens.

- If you are turning up at the venue the day before an event, check the materials when there is still time to act. A quick call to a courier firm can get a box or briefcase sent up overnight, at a very reasonable price. Naturally, this has never happened to me!

- If you are arriving just before a course starts, carry printed sets of the handouts you need in the first hour. Everything after that you should be able to get printed on site from the master set which you are also carrying . . . of course.

'Sorry, I can't help you on the course after all'

When your co-trainer drops out, perhaps because of illness, business or family needs you have three options:

- *Grin and bear it* – in which case, know all the materials and prepare the other sessions as early as you can.
- *Get someone else* – have a contingency trainer. If they can't do everything your (former) colleague could, they should be able to facilitate certain parts. This takes some of the heat off you between sessions.
- *Postpone the course* – sometimes it's better to leave it to a time when you can have your perfect course, rather than merely a passable one.

'Oh no we won't' (oh yes you will . . . please)

What happens if participants refuse to do something? For some trainers it means major loss of face. But for the perfect trainer it gives an opportunity to review the learning methods with the group. Why have they refused? Is it perceived lack of safety? Is it boredom – they've done it before? Do they see the value in the activity?

Ask the group 'what has stopped you wanting to take part in the activity?' By framing the problem as external to them you also have the opportunity to rebuild commitment in your proposal if they didn't understand it. If you phrase it as 'why won't you do it?' you are framing the problem as internal motivation. They'll come up with all sorts of reasons to justify it. Once they've done that no one would be able to change their minds without looking silly.

Respond to their concerns by demonstrating the value of

the activity. Make it sound interesting and challenging. Make sure they understand it well enough so there are no frightening unknowns in it (unless that is the whole point of it).

You may need to be flexible to create something else or modify your existing design. If you need time to do that, be open with the group. Involve them and get them on your side. Once the activity has been redesigned and clarified to the group the participants will be highly motivated to do it – after all, it is 'their' design.

Thank them for being open with you. It is a good sign that they feel comfortable with you to raise such a tricky issue, rather than half-heartedly going on with it and thereby undermining it.

'Good heavens is that the time!'

When an activity or discussion starts running horribly over time it can have all sorts of knock-on effects. The course may finish later. You may not be able to complete a task and fail to achieve the objective. Your session may run into the next person's session. There are two main causes for overruns:

- lack of planning
- lack of control

Planning

Follow the rules of project management when calculating time-scales. If an exercise is new to you, add on some time to it. If the participants are unknown, add some more. If the exercise is complex, add some more again. Then as the task commences, make sure you monitor and control it.

Control

Unless you share time control with participants it is you who are responsible for managing the time. If a participant has a question they will ask it, even if you are already half an hour over time. They will assume that it is all right, that if you have not closed things down then you must have planned it.

The answer is to share control and responsibility for time-keeping with the participants. Tell them how long you have got for a session. Give them deadlines to complete things and help them achieve those deadlines by reminding them about time remaining.

A word of warning: beware making timekeeping appear to be the only factor. I once ran a course with a trainer who used a digital watch alarm to time everything. As the time came up for completion, the alarm sounded – 'beep, beep, beep'. The participants got so annoyed with it they awarded the trainer with a watch with a six-inch nail driven through it. A cruel joke, but a very direct message.

'Sorry to interrupt, can Mr Smith take an urgent call?' (or 'Is that mobile phone of yours ringing?')

Courses on-site can be a nightmare. People may be called away for emergency meetings, or will tell switchboard that they can be paged or rung. Some people can switch off from work and focus on a course; others have a more but-terfly approach and whilst they are there in body, part of their mind is elsewhere.

Equally, courses in a hotel or conference centre can be interrupted, but the venue usually prevents certain ones coming through. Make sure that the hotel knows how to handle calls and that they post the messages outside the room as soon as they come in. Poor message-taking is what often forces participants to start using their mobile phones.

If you have no choice but to run a course on-site make sure that participants know the start and end times, plus the break times. Arrange for someone outside the training room to take messages. In the joining instructions tell participants the number for messages and that sessions won't be interrupted. Messages will be given to them in the breaks for returning in the breaks. Reinforce this at the beginning of the course and ask people with mobile phones to set them to take messages and for others to turn down their pagers.

Don't forget to turn yours off too!

Difficult participants (or 'Where do all these dreadful people come from?')

You've planned perfectly; the materials and exercises have been produced beautifully; the programme has started on time. All would be wonderful if it wasn't for the participants!

I have found most participants to be interesting and delightful people. But inevitably, when you get a group of people together there are some who don't gel with the group, or behave in ways that are disruptive to others' learning.

These are the people who give less experienced trainers, and sometimes us old hacks, grief.

Mocking Bird (A person who mocks the course content, the methods, or you.)

Don't be so relaxed that you lose control. Try jokes to disperse the tension, but don't respond by further mockery. Mockers may be trying to seek attention, but are unable to express their needs. Speak to the person outside the classroom rather than embarrass them. Tell them how their behaviour is affecting you and the course. Ask them in what ways the course could be more helpful to them. Then try to form an agreement to offer them that help provided they behave in the way that would be more cooperative with you.

Quiet mouse

Withdrawn people – or those who just don't say anything – can be hard to spot sometimes, especially if they appear to be listening and look interested during lectures. But when they come to be joined with others in syndicates, their non-participation stands out like a sore thumb. It can affect others; it can certainly make it hard to give them any feedback, other than: 'Well, you didn't say anything, so my judgement is based on your body language'!

For genuinely quiet people, you may just have to remember to involve them and act as gatekeeper, e.g. 'What do you think, Sam?'

You can also try to use methods that involve them, e.g. everyone has a turn to speak; or putting them into pairs or trios with other quiet people. Find out what is getting in the way of their speaking out. Value their contributions – tell them their views are really important to you and how they can help the group.

Dominator

The dominator(s) may be extreme in their views, interrupt everyone (including you), or just go on, and on, and on . . .

You can pair them with other strong characters, leaving other weaker ones to have time to speak and discuss things. You can put them into small groups where they can dominate just a few, and then appoint another group member as their spokesperson. Make sure you change the groups so you don't inflict them on the same people.

You can encourage others to speak. This is better than telling the dominator to shut up.

You can be more specific with your questions, and more specific with what responses you want from the group, e.g. 'Everyone write down two problems they have, using no more than ten words each, and be ready to call them out in three minutes.'

Cynical
Whether you see cynicism as pessimism or just realism, it can often drag down a group's energy. One participant is manageable. Encourage them to look at the positives and the benefits of things. If they are undergoing a change and are at the anger or denial stage, let them talk it out with you off-line. This may not be the best time for them to attend the course.

If the cynicism is among several participants it may be due to something that has happened. I ran a course once in which the managers were feeling angry and stressed. The organization had imposed a new internal market on them, and the resulting turmoil had made it very hard for them to focus on the course. They wanted to be there, but a big black cloud was hanging over all of them.

You can't just ignore their situations. Acknowledge them and let people talk about how they are affected. If it is possible, ask them if they would like to use these situations as part of the course. This needs both flexibility and discipline. The discussion needs to be managed and the changes required to the day's timetable agreed with the group. Otherwise there is a danger that the discussion has no end, or gets reopened at every opportunity.

Know-all (or 'Been there, done that, bought the T-shirt')
Someone who knows more than you do (or believes they do) can feel quite threatening. But unless they are mocking, a know-all probably just wants their experience recognized.

Get them on your side. If you haven't already, ask them what they hope to get from the course. Acknowledge their experience and tell them that you will appreciate their help in working with the others. And let them tell their war stories at an appropriate time. For other participants who are inexperienced, ask them questions before asking the more experienced member.

Equally, don't let all that 'experience' be an excuse to avoid doing activities. They may be worried that some greenhorn will be better than them. But if they are there to learn, challenge them if they don't get involved.

'They're alive, Jim, but not as we know it'

Sometimes a group appears dead and unresponsive. Impassive faces greet your jokes, a wonderful presentation results in no signs of illumination, or nobody answers your questions.

The reasons for this happening may vary depending on when it happens. At the beginning of a course, they may be getting their bearings or be scared. What do you still need to do to establish a good learning climate?

After (a heavy) lunch they may be just tired and sleepy. Something may have happened back at work? Or to one of the participants? Ask them. Find out why the group isn't responding. See the notes under planning for buzz groups, energizers and questions in chapter 7.

Other behaviours

If you have other behaviours which you are finding difficulty with, try the three Rs of preventing unfair tactics in negotiating:

Recognize it	Noticing the behaviour and being able to describe it is crucial. You can't negotiate a grievance, but you can negotiate for the sort of behaviour you would like instead.
Raise it	Bring it up with the person, preferably in private so you can discuss the impact of

their behaviour. Quite often, 'difficult' participants don't recognize themselves as such. When told they are horrified, and change instantly.

Re-negotiate it Tell them what you would like them to do instead; and if necessary any consequences of their not co-operating. If this prevents them from learning so effectively, discuss what you might be able to do to help them.

9

'HOW DID I DO?' – EVALUATING YOUR COURSE

When you go on a course, you are almost always asked to fill in a course evaluation form. Why? The cynic might say that the form shows participants that the trainers care. Or it's a way of finishing the programme. Many trainers call these forms 'happy sheets' – the participants are ready to leave, perhaps pleased they have survived the rigors of the last few days, or feeling that they have passed the test and become one of a club. If they feel all that, how accurate will their evaluation be?

Nevertheless, happy sheets continue to be used. Trainers use them because they are easy to administer and provide some useful information on the immediate impressions of a course. But there may be more information to be discovered . . .

This chapter looks at:

- Some of the benefits of evaluating training in an organization
- Whether it is worth doing anything else other than happy sheets
- The methods that might be most suitable for the course you are doing

BENEFITS OF EVALUATING TRAINING

An evaluation can answer questions covering the impact of a course on an organization, to the effectiveness of a trainer. Five questions which you may want to get answered are:

1   Have the participants learned what they were meant to have learned?
2   Were the training methods and trainers effective?

3   Were participants able to transfer the learned skills or
     knowledge to their work?
4   Did these new skills or use of knowledge make a dif-
     ference to the participants' effectiveness in their job?
5   Did that increased effectiveness have an impact on the
     business in line with its business goals?

The five questions follow an increasing level of difficulty in
uncovering the answer. It is relatively easy to check on a
course whether someone can do what has just been demonstrated, or can answer a question on what has been
discussed. But it may be hard to say for certain whether a
course has had a measurable impact on the business objectives.

The different questions look at different parts of the training process.

Questions 1 and 2 look at the *internal design and delivery*
process. It is rare for these not to be asked, as most trainers
like to have some feedback for improvements. But what if
a course has been set up to help people mix with other
departments and to find out what they do? Is an evaluation
worthwhile?

Question 3 looks at *learning transfer issues*. If a course is for
career development there is little point considering it. If it
is for job needs, then it is extremely pertinent.

Question 4 looks at the *training needs analysis*. If the course
was designed to improve working methods then it would
be an appropriate question to get responses to. If the training was for general skills, or for the next job move, it cannot
be immediately answered.

Question 5 looks at the *links between the course purpose and
objectives, and the organizational goals*. If a course has been set
up for individual development reasons such as career

development, there may be few links with the organizational goals.

You may decide what you want to evaluate according to your interest or your uncertainty about what you have got right and what you haven't. There are other ways of deciding, and the next section explores these.

HOW MUCH EFFORT SHOULD YOU PUT INTO EVALUATION?

Some of the questions below might help you work out if evaluation is worthwhile and to what degree you should go about your evaluation. There more 'yes' answers you have, the greater the value you will derive from evaluation and the more effort you may wish to put into it.

- Is the cost of training high, either in cash or time? A low-cost course rarely merits a large amount of time spent in data collection or reporting back to management.
- What is the level of support within the organization for training or a training function? Evaluation can provide valuable ammunition to maintain training – assuming the evaluation is good of course!
- Will the course be repeated? If a course is a one-off, evaluation has less value to future participants on courses.
- Do the trainers need detailed feedback for their own development? A trainer who has delivered the same course many times will get less value from feedback. New trainers on a long-standing course or experienced trainers on a new course will be able to use the feedback to improve their performance next time.
- Do you want to improve relationships with line managers by involving them in course evaluation?
- Do you have sufficient resources to collate information, analyse it and create an evaluation report from it?
- Is this a strategically important course? A customer

services course in a service company may be; a job-hunting course for redundant managers may not.
- Are there existing methods of measuring job performance which might make data collection easier.

If you scored **7–8** then you need to take a long hard look at what you need to evaluate. Chances are that training is a key part of the organization's future, but it may be under threat. Use the suggestions below for methods of evaluation and build support for it.

If you scored **4–6** then certain types of evaluation might be worth considering. You need to decide what stage of the training process you need to evaluate. The questions you answered 'yes' to will give you an indication.

If you scored **1–3** then some limited evaluation may be useful. Even if you only use happy sheets, consider how you can make the most of them.

HOW CAN YOU EVALUATE?
This section covers some useful approaches to evaluation, the problems of each, and how you might go about using them.

Course evaluation forms (happy sheets)
These give trainers useful feedback about the reactions of participants immediately after a course. They are a subjective measure of the content and the process of the course, and the relative usefulness of the material.

Problems
Sometimes participants may be influenced by one good or one bad event. The influence of these factors is known as the *halo* or *horns* effect. Participants influenced by the halo effect of one excellent factor may notice only the other good things and ignore the bad. Participants influenced by the horns effect of one bad factor make everything seem worse.

For example, course reactions can be affected by the entertainment value of the course and the trainer. In the UK and USA a trainer who can crack jokes and win the support of participants can score highly on both content and process issues, whereas a more serious-minded trainer may not. In many Far Eastern countries, a trainer who has put participants in an awkward position may find that the content has scored poorly, even though it is the trainer's style at fault. In Germany, jokes are less valued in business, so too much levity will undermine the course.

Another problem with asking for reactions at the end of a course involves the *primacy* and *recency* effects. People remember most what happened at the beginning or the end. This is why most trainers want to make sure a course starts off well and finishes with a flourish. Following this with an evaluation may cause participants to be heavily influenced by the ending and to some extent, the beginning. But the guts of the course, the middle, has been forgotten or given less emphasis.

Evaluation forms can be difficult to analyse and report on. Although comments are useful for design aspects, they require time to collate and type up. One of my clients used to have participants e-mail in their evaluations after the course. The resulting impressions varied from a few words to pages. This is a learner-centred way of evaluating and works well providing it is the individuals who are influencing the course design and content. The results could not be used for improving future courses because other participants would have different needs.

Giving out evaluation forms and asking participants to send them in once they have had a chance to consider a course can often result in a low response rate. Often it is the participants who feel negatively about a course who reply – the happy punters don't bother. This can give the false impression that the course is universally disliked. Chasing up non-returned forms can be an administrative headache.

Advantages

Because of their immediacy they are good at evaluating the process of the course. Months later participants should remember the learning points but may not remember how a topic was covered. This is why trainers like happy sheets as a means of evaluation – they are good at giving feedback about the trainers' skills. An evaluation form is easy to administer and relatively simple to design.

Tips

To overcome immediate post-course euphoria and the halo and horns effect you can ask participants to fill in their evaluation form as they go along. For a course with a number of inputs from different people, have an evaluation after each session. You might even have separate forms for each session.

Use scoring scales for the various different aspects you want to evaluate. This makes the task of collating results easier. It also gives the reporting back of results a more scientific feel. Beware of over-analyzing scores. Because of the subjectivity of participants using this method a deviation of a few points from one course to the next is rarely significant.

To make rating scales more accurate, you can give examples at either end. Behaviourally-anchored rating scales (BARS) tell participants what the extremes would represent. A rating scale with a central example gives even more guidance. For example, a scale for 'trainer presentation' might be:

1	5	10
Unclear, unstructured, no links to other sessions. Did not appear to understand material.	Wandered at times, some links with previous points, knew main thrust of subject but unable to answer harder questions.	Well structured, speaks clearly and concisely, clarifies messages, links back and forth to other material. Has an excellent grasp of material.

A typical post-course evaluation form is shown in appendix A.

For a course lasting a day or more, pass out forms at the beginning and encourage participants to make notes as they go along. Mention the benefit that this will mean less of a rush for them at the end.

Ask participants to complete their forms and hand them in before they leave. This ensures a full response. Providing it is coupled with handing out forms in advance, participants won't be too rushed to complete it thoroughly.

Another variation of forms is to ask participants to fill in post-it notes under various headings which you supply, then ask them to post them onto a flip chart with the headings already on it. This feels more informal and allows participants to view their colleagues' feedback without being influenced by it. Analyzing the patterns is slightly easier as all comments can be viewed in one go.

Discussion at end of course
If you don't want to ask participants to put pen to paper, or you want to get details that a written evaluation might not capture, you can ask them to *discuss* their views.

Problems
Most dominant participants might overly influence the

group's views; other members who hold different views may either keep quiet or change their own view. Participants who have been helped may still be reluctant to admit weaknesses in public.

There are similar problems of halo/horns and primacy/recency, as with post-course evaluation forms.

Advantages
A discussion is quick and immediate, so it is good for looking at the process of how the course was run. The points can be easily summarized. Discussion shows participants that their views are valued, providing trainers take the feedback well (don't argue or excuse). The variation of closing circle (see below) is a positive way of closing a course and disbanding a group.

Tips
Group discussion – Break the group into sub-groups who discuss the course and report back. This partially overcomes problems of dominant members. However, make sure that each spokesperson is instructed to represent *all* their members' views – you are not looking for consensus. Try to appoint people who will not dominate the discussion.

Closing circle – Another variation is the 'closing circle' which asks each participant in turn to say something about the course and its impact on them. Items included are:

- What (one/two/three things) will you be taking away in your kitbag?
- What did you value most about being on the course?
- What one thing did you really find useful and what one thing would you change about the course?

Closing circles often focus on the positive outcomes of a course. This enables participants to leave feeling good about it. To retain data a trainer normally has to note down all the points, so this technique is often reserved for when there is another trainer, or someone who can take accurate notes.

Questionnaires to look at post-course change

A questionnaire seeks to uncover what has been remembered or implemented after the course. As such there are different purposes of questionnaires:

- as a test of what is remembered of the tuition (*knowledge recall*)
- a survey of what behaviour has changed on the job (*behaviour skills transfer*)
- a survey of what parts of the course were useful (*evaluation of training needs analysis*)

It is sent out after a course, sometimes weeks or months later. Evaluation questionnaires are best designed at the same time as the course. They should include the main objectives of the course. There are two main structures for questionnaires:

1 multiple choice
2 open questions inviting free-form responses

Problems

Questionnaires are time-consuming to design, complete, and analyse. They may suffer from poor response rates. Unless you are doing a lot of the same training a number of times, the course is of great business significance, or the data would be valuable in some other way (e.g. bolstering the reputation of training), they may not be worth the effort.

Advantages

Questionnaires provide a better quality analysis of course content than happy sheets or discussion. This is principally because they show what happens over time and can examine whether skills or knowledge are being used on the job.

Tips
Multiple-choice questionnaires – These make scoring of questionnaires easier for the administrator. The answers have to be right or wrong. They can be used either for tests or for feedback where you want to constrain possible responses to make scoring easier. For example:

1   Questionnaires can be used for (tick those which are correct):

a testing what is remembered of a course   ❐

b looking at the ways in which skills can be
   applied   ❐

c giving trainers useful feedback of what they
   did right   ❐

or

1   The skill of summarizing has been useful when (tick those which are correct):

a taking customer orders   ❐

b appraising staff   ❐

c negotiating with customers   ❐

d planning a day   ❐

- Check that the items are a representative sample of the course and do not wrongly emphasize any learning points.
- If any learning points are more important, give them a suitable weighting in the scoring.
- Check that all the questions are understandable by piloting the questionnaire and getting feedback on it.

- Check all the answers are also understandable and can't be misinterpreted.
- Answers should not have any grey areas, they should be right or wrong.
- Don't mix questions that test for knowledge with those that ask about application of skills.

Open questions inviting free-form responses – Free-form, or qualitative, questionnaires allow the respondent to answer a question in any way they like. They are slightly easier to design, but harder to analyse. Because of the freedom of response they can provide richer data about the course and about the application of skills in the job.

A good example of a free-form question is:

In what situations have you been able to apply the skill of summarizing points?

When writing questions make sure they are not so loose that they can be interpreted in many ways. For example, had the last question been phrased as:

How have you been able to use the skill of summarizing points?

This could have been interpreted in too many ways. It could mean *what has motivated* you to use the skill, it could mean *where* have you used it, or *what technique* has helped you to use it.

Again it is useful to pilot a questionnaire on colleagues or past participants before using it more widely.

Focus Groups
Focus groups are generally after a course. They can bring together samples of past participants, or the various 'stakeholders' involved in the course. These may include participants, trainers, course designers, line managers,

training managers, senior managers. A focus group process is similar to the discussion method, except it also aims to look at the course evaluation from the various different perspectives that the group's members bring.

Problems

Focus groups can be hard to assemble, to co-ordinate the time of many interested parties. Because of the trainer's involvement it may be hard for them to facilitate such a meeting. Equally not all the people impacted by a course may *want* to attend.

The evaluations resulting from focus groups are more subjective than some survey methods. They depend on the members' accuracy of description and recall. By choosing different focus group members the result can vary. For example, a manager who looks favourably on training may attribute more benefits to a course than a dubious manager.

Advantages

Focus groups are a quick way to gain an understanding of the opinions of a sample of people.

The attendees of focus groups often feel more involved in the training course they are discussing. It raises their awareness of changes that have happened. This makes a focus group a good way of building commitment to training from senior and line managers.

Tips

Have a limited number of people involved in a focus group. Set aside no more than an hour in a quiet room.

Let them know what the objective of the meeting is, e.g. 'to identify the changes amongst your staff that have resulted from recent information technology training, and to evaluate the resulting impact on the organization'.

Facilitate their views and record them on a flip chart, or have someone else taking notes of the key points. Have the notes typed up later so you can circulate them to the participants with the conclusions of the exercise.

An example set of questions to prompt discussion would be:

1   What have you noticed your staff doing differently after the course?
2   Can you give examples of what they have been able to do?
3   What are they still not able to do which you expected them to be capable of?
4   What was the impact on your operations as a result of this?
5   What is the value to the organization of this training?

Course follow-ups

Follow-ups enable participants to reinforce their learning by meeting again some weeks after a course for a day or half-day. At a follow-up, the participants normally discuss what problems they have had using some of the ideas or skills they have learned, what they can recall, and what they still need to learn. The trainer needs to be flexible and to add in other ideas which may help learning transfer.

Problems

Because the focus of the follow-up is support, the gathering of data for evaluation purposes can be harder. Participants may not be as honest about their problems in front of their group as they would be for a survey.

Reforming a complete group can be difficult. Missing members, who may have left the organization, or be doing 'more important work', leave a hole in the group. But mixing up members from several courses also has problems – they have to get to know one another, which extends the length of the follow-up.

Advantages
Although the purpose of a follow-up is usually one of supporting the learning, by its nature, a lot of information is gained which can assist evaluation of training.

It gives the trainer an idea about what parts of the course worked well and what didn't. Participants discuss what was easy and what was difficult to implement back at work.

Tips
Research before the follow-up can help in preparation; it may also give evaluation data which you would not otherwise gain during the follow-up itself.

Treat the follow-up as though it is a separate course, but make sure the needs analysis is done after the initial course.

To reduce drop-out levels for a follow-up, book the date early and advise participants at the time of organizing the first course.

FURTHER HELP

Useful addresses

Video and other materials
Pba Training Services
2 Paul Street
London EC2A 4JH
0171 375 3775

European Case Clearing House
Cranfield University
Wharley End
Bedford MK43 0JR
01234 750903

Conference venue finders
Hotel Brokers
19 Bakery Place
119 Altenburg Gardens
London SW11 1JQ
0171 924 3663

Conference Search
1st Floor
92 Church Lane
Marple
Cheshire SK6 7AR
0161 427 7057

Trainer tuition and qualifications
Institute of Personnel Development
IPD House
Camp Road, Wimbledon
London SW19 4UX
0181 971 9000

Bibliography and Further Reading

Bramley, Peter, *Evaluating Training Effectiveness* (London, McGraw-Hill, 1991)

Buzan, Tony, *Use Your Head* (London, BBC Publications, 1974) In the USA, entitled *Use Both Sides of Your Brain* (New York, E. P. Duton, 1977)

Goldstein, Irwin L., *Training in Organizations* (California, Brooks/Cole Publishing, 1986)

Hofstede, Geert, 'Motivation, Leadership and Organization: Do American Theories Apply Abroad?' in *Organization Theory*, edited by D. S. Pugh (London, Penguin, 1990)

Honey, Peter, and Alan Mumford, *Manual of Learning Styles* (Peter Honey, 1992)

Kelly, John, Eugene Donnelly and Margaret Reid, *Manpower Training and Development* (London, IPM, 1983)

O'Connor, Joseph, and John Seymour, *Training With NLP* (London, Thorsons, 1994)

APPENDIX A
SPECIMEN FEEDBACK SHEET

Your feedback is appreciated for continued improvement of our training courses. Please be as detailed as possible in your comments.

Course Design & Content

How well were the stated course objectives met?

0   5

NOT AT ALL   FULLY

Comments:

Which aspects were most useful?

What should there be more of?

What should there be less of?

How good were the handouts/materials?

0   5

POOR   VERY GOOD

Comments:

The Individual

How well were your personal course objectives met?

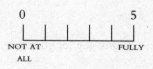

0   5

NOT AT ALL   FULLY

Comments:

What will you do differently as a result of this course?

What further development needs have you identified?

Admin and Venue

How good was the pre-course
administration? (e.g. enquiries,
joining instructions, bookings)
Comments:

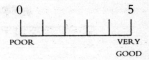

How suitable was the venue?
Comments:

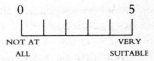

Trainers/Facilitators

Please comment on the individual style(s) of the trainer(s).

Name of trainer/facilitator:
Comments:

Name of trainer/facilitator:
Comments:

Name of trainer/facilitator:
Comments:

Any Other Comments

Thank you for your time.

Signed (optional) . . . .

N.B. Individual views will not be attributed. Your name
helps us understand your feedback better.

APPENDIX B

Preparation Checklist
The checklist items are covered in chronological order, though for some large scale events or for short notice events this may vary.

- Aims and Objectives set
- Objectives agreed with main sponsors
- Evaluation methods planned and agreed
- Course sessions planned
- Handouts
  - Writing
  - Proof reading
  - Printing and Binding
- Trainer notes written
- Team briefing of trainers
- Overheads or slides produced
- Venue identified
- Map and travel details for venue and its contact numbers for calls to participants
- Venue advised of:
  - Main room and syndicate rooms layout
  - Equipment needs
  - Meal menus, and coffee and tea and times
  - Message taking procedures
  - Final rooming lists of participants and trainers
- Joining instructions sent to participants, including:
  - Start and finish times
  - Course objectives or aims
  - Pre-course requirements
  - Map and travel details
  - Telephone and fax contact numbers while at venue
  - Procedure for reclaiming expenses
  - Dress codes
  - Dietary requirements – who to contact

- Contact participants to discuss their objectives
- Pack and send boxes with materials, slides, equipment, and stationery, including:
  - Ring binders, name tents, lapel badges, pens or pencils, writing pads, spare acetates and acetate pens, flip chart pads and pens, hole puncher, stapler and staple remover, Blu-tac or masking tape
- Set up and test equipment on site in time to arrange for standby if necessary.